Angels Watching Over Us

IN THE SHADOW OF WINGS

ANNE BROYLES
REBECCA CHRISTIAN
CAROL MCADOO REHME
CAROL SMITH
DIANA L. THRIFT
NATALIE WALKER W̶

Publications International, Ltd.

Louis Weber, CEO
Publications International, Ltd.
7373 North Cicero Avenue
Lincolnwood, Illinois 60712

Permission is never granted for commercial purposes.

Manufactured in USA.

8 7 6 5 4 3 2 1

ISBN: 0-7853-9316-1

CONTENTS

ABIDING ANGELS

A ngels. You may have heard them on high, played one in a Christmas pageant, prayed to your guardian angels, or sung hymns in praise of cherubim and seraphim.

We've all admired Christmas cards and the classic paintings of white-robed angels in human form, with their gossamer wings and halos bathing their beautiful faces in golden light.

But angels exist at all times, not just at Christmas. They don't always fly into our lives with a flourish of trumpets and a rustle of wings, streaming radiance. They aren't always pretty: Remember Clarence, the lumpy angel in *It's a Wonderful Life* who finally gets his wings by helping George Bailey?

You may find an angel in the teacher who shows infinite patience to a learning-challenged child or in the tough-talking but tenderhearted nurse who takes care of an elderly parent. You may find an angel in the mechanic who makes your wheezing car safe for yet another thousand miles. You may encounter an angel in the beautician who listens sympathetically while she's cutting your hair and even offers some coping strategies when you tell her about your problems.

Your mother or father, simply by loving you and teaching you by example, may have been the first angels in your life. Children and grandchildren, with their sticky kisses and warm, trusting hands they put in yours, may be little angels caring for you.

Even in those times when we cannot see or sense them—perhaps especially in those times—angels are still there, accompanying us. In *Angels Watching Over Us,* you will find a host of stories about how angels affect people's lives in myriad ways and in many forms, including guardian angels, angels in uniform, messenger angels, guiding angels, animal angels, and angels of peace who lift us up on wings of hope.

Like many people who come to believe in angels, you may have already discovered that the best way to find your angel is to be one. As the Bible says, "Do not neglect to show hospitality to strangers, for by doing that some have entertained angels without knowing it" (Hebrews 13:2).

GUARDIAN ANGELS

We never travel alone.
Invisible angels surround us,
walking with us on our journey,
quietly sustaining our spirits,
pouring love over us
with the lightness of air—
and we don't even hear the
rustling of their wings.

If you pray truly, you will feel within yourself a
great assurance: and the angels will be your
companions.

EVAGRIUS OF PONTUS

THE VOICE OF CALM

As much as Miranda loved being home with her children, she welcomed the occasional road trips her consultant work involved. Early one November morning as she finished packing for a trip, gripes erupted from her three kids. Taylor refused to put on the "itchy" pants Miranda had laid out for her to wear to preschool. Jordan said his scrambled eggs were "too wet." An entire gallon of milk had disappeared since the day before. Sighing eloquently, Miranda called her faithful baby-sitter, Mrs. Wilmot, and asked if she could pick up some milk on her way over.

A profound sense of relief enveloped Miranda as she headed out to the highway. It cut through the picturesque valley of the river on which her pretty small town was set. She tuned the radio to a soft-rock station, chilled out, and sang along.

When she was a half-hour out of town, she slowed down at a sign that warned curves were ahead. Negotiating a steep incline, she hit an unexpected patch of ice while at the same time her brain registered a car up ahead, rolled over in the ditch. In the split second in which she could react, her overpowering impulse was to slam on the brakes with all her might. Yet she heard a familiar voice in her head saying, "Stay calm. Turn in the direction of the skid." It was the voice of her fuddy-duddy driver's education teacher, whose safety rules had driven her crazy.

Her car skidded in slow motion and then slid ever so gently into the ditch, stopping just a few inches from the overturned car. Within moments, a highway patrol officer came along. Miranda assured him that she was fine, and he summoned the tow truck that pulled her car out of the ditch. Meanwhile, the sun had risen and the slippery patch of ice had vanished.

Miranda drove home, anxious to hold her precious children. When she burst in the door, the kids were so engrossed in a game of Candyland with Mrs. Wilmot that they barely returned her fervent hugs. That night as Miranda said her prayers, she didn't know what she was more thankful for—the persistent voice of her driver's ed teacher, whom she now

considered her guardian angel for reminding
her how to handle slippery roads, or the
reminder of what's most important in life.

*The guardian angels of life sometimes fly
so high as to be beyond our sight, but they
are always looking down upon us.*

JEAN PAUL RICHTER

*How gentle are the whispers of my
    Guardian Angel dear,
How kindly are the promptings, ever
    faithful, always near;
How soft is the voice that calms and
    quiets all my fear,
How peaceful is the feeling that the road
    ahead is clear,
How quiet is the counsel that my heart
    alone can hear.*

A Stranger's Story

The checkout clerk at the discount department store stifled a yawn as she gave Jane a tired smile. Jane felt herself begin to yawn. "Wow, I guess it's catching!" she commented as both women laughed.

"Sorry," the clerk said. "I was up all night and started here early."

"Well, I hope it was for something good," Jane said lightly, as she put the last of her purchases on the counter. When she looked at the clerk more carefully, though, she doubted it, because the look the other woman wore was one of resignation.

"No, it was for something bad," she said quietly, not raising her eyes from the items she scanned.

"Well, I'm sorry," Jane said, "and I didn't mean to pry."

At the sincerity in Jane's voice, the other woman looked up, "Oh, that's okay," she said. "I was in the emergency room with a friend who tried to kill herself."

"My goodness," Jane exclaimed.

"Yeah, it was pretty scary, but she's okay now," the woman said ruefully. "Well, you know…I hope she can get some help…"

"She's lucky you were there to help," Jane said.

"She called me before she lost consciousness. I guess she didn't really want to do it after all."

"I guess she had an angel watching over her," Jane said, feeling relief for the sake of a stranger whose story she had been privileged to hear. It was then she noticed on the woman's shirt the name tag "Gabriella."

"Why, it's you, you're her angel," Jane said, staring at the name tag. "Gabriella—you're even named after an angel!"

Slowly, the tired look on Gabriella's face changed into a smile. "That's right," she said slowly, "I'd forgotten all about that."

The two women smiled warmly at their shared discovery. For even better than recognizing a guardian angel in others is realizing that angel in yourself.

*How many angels are there? One—who
transforms our life—is plenty.*

TRADITIONAL SAYING

><+>-O-<+>-<

*Guardian angels God will send thee
All through the night.*

SIR HAROLD BOULTON

TEEN ANGEL

Something roused Nina from sleep. One of
the children coughing? With her husband
away on business, until tonight she hadn't slept
well all week. "Just when I'm finally getting a
good night's...Oh, well," Nina grumbled as
she tossed aside the covers and slid into her
slippers. "I'll just do a quick room check."
When she opened her bedroom door, acrid
smoke billowed in.

"Mama!"

Which one of her two children was calling? She
felt her way down the hall, palming the wall
from side to side, bumping her hip on the sharp
corner of the bookshelf. Smoke stung her eyes.

It burned her nose and clogged her throat.

"Leslie?"

"Mama!"

"Leslie, grab my hand and don't let go. We've got to get to your brother."

"No, Mama, no. Remember? We're supposed to crawl."

Thank goodness for the preschool's fire safety training, Nina thought. *Of course* they should drop down where the air was not so dense with smoke. With Leslie clasping a knotted corner of Nina's long nightgown, they crawled around the corner.

"Evan," she rasped. "Evan, where are you?" Was it her imagination or was the smoke thicker here?

"I'm sorry, I'm sorry, Mom!" he sobbed.

"What? I can't see you. I can barely hear you. Where are you?"

"In here. The fire! Mom, help me. I didn't mean to. I just borrowed the lighter. Mom!" Evan choked.

The fire was on the other side of the door, between her and Evan. Nina strained to recall what she could about fire survival. Thinking quickly, she tugged her daughter toward the living room and yelled, "Evan, stand by your window. I'll be right back!"

"But, Mama," Leslie objected.

"Hush and don't let go. Hurry!"

Somehow, Nina managed to get Leslie out of the house and to the sidewalk by the street. By then, smoke rolled from the roof, and flames erupted from the house.

"Evan!" she screamed, racing around the outer corner to his bedroom window.

"Don't worry. I'll get him."

Startled, Nina looked over her shoulder. It was the lanky, long-haired biker who lived down the street, the same teenager she urged her children to avoid. He was hard-looking, with purple spiked hair, tattoos, and profuse piercings.

"Get back!" he ordered both Nina and Evan. With no thought for himself, he broke the window, knocked away the shattered glass with his leather-gloved hands, and pulled Evan through the window of the burning building. He handed the boy to his mother.

Nina was shocked: The man in denim and earrings was a hero. Then she noticed that the glow of the flames shooting up behind him was perfectly framing his face. At that moment, it looked like he was wearing a halo. This young man was an angel—he was her angel!

PRAYER FOR PROTECTION

Protect us all and keep us safe,
Help us find our way.
Show us light and make us wise,
Keep the wolves at bay.
Help us not to limit our trust to doors and
        locks and shrill alarms,
Help us rest in angels' strong and
        ever-present arms.

ANGEL BUDDY

Cautiously, Lynn Spinner eased her truck and trailer into the stream of traffic leaving town for the holiday weekend. Her daughters chattered happily in the cab, excited about the weekend of camping and horseback riding with friends in the wooded hills of northeast Iowa.

"Too bad Daddy has to coach that darn judo tournament in Chicago and can't come with us, huh, Mom?" remarked 14-year-old Joanna.

"Yep, too bad for him, he'll miss the beauty of nature as seen from the back of a fine horse!" Lynn teased. "We'll miss him, but luckily we girls are adventurers, right?"

The bravado was as much for herself as for the children, though Lynn wasn't worried about the camping or trail riding part of the trip. Yet Lynn knew she wouldn't be able to relax until she'd pulled safely into the campground and turned off the ignition. Whenever she had to haul horses—which was usually just a few miles down to 4-H practices—she felt the weighty responsibility of all the lives, both human and equine, that were in her hands. Before setting out with the trailer, Lynn always said a quick prayer, asking for protection for her family and animals.

As usual, after about 30 miles, Lynn pulled off at a little rest stop. "I just want to make sure everything's all right." The girls rolled their eyes and skipped off to the candy machine, returning just as Lynn finished checking the tire pressure.

"Mom, you already did that once today!" Joanna chided.

Chiming in, 11-year-old Sophie exclaimed, "Mom, you're such a worrier!"

Yes, I am, she thought, and resolved to lighten up; after all, her mechanic had recently checked the vehicle and said all was well.

A half hour later, they were cruising down a long hill toward the Cedar River. Out of the corner of her eye, she saw a white pickup truck speed up then slow down beside them in the next lane. How irritating. Suddenly Joanna shouted, "Mom, he wants us to pull over, we have a flat!"

Carefully, Lynn slowed the speeding rig and eased onto the shoulder. The white pickup pulled over, too, and out jumped a man. "Lock the doors and stay in the truck," she told her daughters as she stepped out.

"Your tire is coming apart all over the highway!" yelled the man as he headed to the rear trailer tire.

Lynn was speechless when she saw it—all the rubber was gone around the middle, and a section of tread lay in the road.

"It's a wonder it didn't blow," the man said. "Do you have a trailer jack and a spare?"

"Yes," she said, nodding her head.

"Good, that'll make it easier. I'll get the tools from my truck."

"You mean we can change it here? What about the horses?" She looked doubtfully at the steep bank on one side and the heavy traffic whizzing by on the other.

"If the horses don't move around and shake the trailer, I'd leave 'em inside. By the way, I'm Bill Buddy," he said.

She couldn't believe how quickly he worked; soon the bad tire was off and the spare was on. Lynn and the girls thanked him profusely, and she offered money for his time and trouble.

"No, no," he said, "Glad I could help. If my wife and kids had a problem on the road, I'd sure hope someone would help them. You ladies have a safe trip!"

As he waved and climbed into his truck, Joanna whispered to her mother, "He must be an angel, huh?"

Lynn hugged her daughters, "Yes. Thank God for angels like Bill Buddy!"

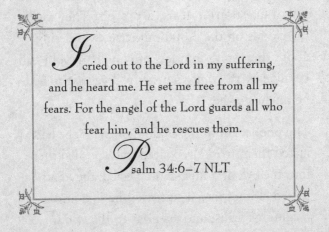

I cried out to the Lord in my suffering, and he heard me. He set me free from all my fears. For the angel of the Lord guards all who fear him, and he rescues them.

*P*salm 34:6–7 NLT

Thank you for the unseen hands that guide my way. Thank you for the eyes that watch my step. Thank you for the care that keeps me safe, even when the angels are incognito. Thank you for the trouble I have missed even though I never saw it coming. Every visible thing in this world is under the charge of an angel.

SAINT AUGUSTINE

A WING AND A PRAYER

They entered the trauma unit holding hands. It had been a long flight to Los Angeles. A silent flight spent gazing over the wing. A flight full of questions...fears...prayers. They raced the clouds on the 2,000-mile trip, wondering about their son's injuries, praying he would still be alive by the time they arrived yet frightened he might not be.

The phone call in the middle of the night had jarred them from deep sleep and spiraled them into the eye of a hurricane. Dazed, they had tossed clothes into a suitcase, the dog into a neighbor's arms, and agendas to the wind.

Rushing, rushing, rushing to be with their first-born son, Brad.

Bright, witty, kind-hearted. Newly graduated from college. Serving at an inner-city mission with a bright future at his fingertips and . . . now critically injured by a drunk driver. He was the victim of a hit-and-run.

Their church's senior pastor had kindly called ahead; strangers escorted them from the airport; doctors met them at the hospital. At last they could finally see their son. With their hearts in their throats, they guarded their emotions and braced themselves.

The trauma unit wasn't a peaceful haven. Monitors beeped. A ventilator pulsed. Medical personnel bustled. A confusing host of wires, tubes, and hoses spun a web, and in its center was their comatose son. They watched luminous lines measuring his heartbeats, every breath a gift. They tried to find a place to touch him, caress him. They tried to lean close enough to tell him they were there, that they loved him, and that he needed to work at staying alive.

Tearfully, they clasped hands across the sterile bed linens covering his body and prayed for enough strength to fight this battle, for the health of their son...for a way to calm their panic. As they opened their eyes, serenity engulfed the room and their hearts. A holy hush muted the beeps, bleeps, and buzzes, and the glow from his lamp suddenly seemed like a godly light encircling the bed.

They felt the presence of guardian angels. Emissaries sent to protect and to comfort. To them it was evidence that God had heard their pleas to safeguard their son. A sacred peace enveloped them and winged its way to their hearts. It was this peace that helped them through the wait for Brad to come to. And when he did awake and begin his long, yet successful rehabilitation process, it was that same peace that gave them the constant strength to encourage and support Brad, feeling his guardian angels would always be there in times of need.

ANGELS ALL AROUND US

There are angels all around us,
No one is alone,
Even in our darkest hour
Our deepest needs are known.
There are angels all around us,
Though we rarely get to see,
The guardians among us,
Watching over you and me.

><

As long as we believe in angels, we are
never lost.

STREET SIGNS

Coming to the city was a mistake. Ellie suspected it before she came and now she had proof. She was a country bumpkin lost among the foreign species in this concrete jungle. What had she been thinking to move here? Traipsing the streets for job interviews, walking upstream through this cold crush of humanity. Pungent smells. Honking horns. Rumbling buses. People of every color and language. A hodgepodge of ethnicity. It was next to impossible to find anyone who spoke English, or spoke English without a thick, indecipherable accent.

Now Ellie was lost. Obviously, she had misread the directions and made a wrong turn. Trying to make sense of her situation, she looked from her crumpled map to the street sign and back again. She glanced down the sidewalk. Where was she?

Buildings were shabbier, some standing empty, others boarded over. Several places had iron grids barring their storefront windows. A brassy street worker whistled a rude comment. Rough-looking teens, some in leather and chains, stared in silence as Ellie walked past.

Her heart thumped. Sweat beaded her upper lip. Increasing her pace, Ellie turned back the way she'd....

Thud.

Bumped off balance by someone behind her, Ellie clung to her precious map.

Thud.

Someone else shoved her to her knees this time and, in one swift motion, grabbed the purse she had dropped. She heard shoes slapping the concrete as they ran away. Gathering her wits, Ellie looked up. One of those rough teens was racing toward her!

He jerked to a stop beside her sprawled form and loomed over her. Ellie cowered and cringed, clasping the crumpled map to her chest.

"Lady? You hurt? Lady, you gonna be okay?"

"Y-yes."

"Don't you worry, lady. One of my boys will find your purse."

Ellie's eyes widened.

"Lady? Can you hear me?" He held out his hand. "Let me help you up."

Confused, Ellie hesitantly placed her delicate hand in his strong hand—and then she smiled at him. She had discovered that guardian angels don't necessarily appear in the image you may expect.

*Father God, teach me to trust your
protection. It's so hard sometimes to find
my way home. The nights get dark. The
clouds hide the stars. If I could learn to
hold the hand of your angels, I know you
would lead me all the way.*

My guardian angel is watching
Over me night and day.
I know whenever I need help,
My angel is just a prayer away.

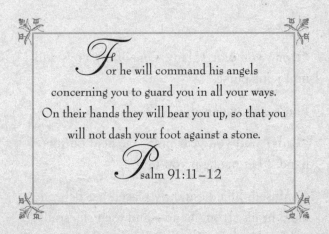

For he will command his angels
concerning you to guard you in all your ways.
On their hands they will bear you up, so that you
will not dash your foot against a stone.

Psalm 91:11–12

LITTLE ANGELS

I believe in angels—
They're around me every day,
I see them in a baby's smile,
And in a child at play.
I hear them in a young girl's call,
And in a newborn's cry;
In a toddler's faltering words,
And in a lullaby.
I see them in big brothers
And big sisters offering care.
I hear them in an infant's laugh,
And in a child's prayer.

⤞•◦•⤝

Love children especially, for like the angels they
too are sinless, and they live to soften and
purify our hearts, and, as it were, to guide us.

FEODOR DOSTOEVSKY

ARRIVING CHICAGO

Bess thanked the flight crew as she disembarked in Chicago. She had taken only a few steps when she felt a crushing pain in her chest. She stopped and leaned forward, bracing herself against the corridor wall as the pressure grew. Then someone grabbed her arm and guided her into the terminal. Bess felt herself being eased into a chair.

She could hardly breathe, and when she raised her eyes she looked into the face of a small girl no older than five.

"Where's your medicine?" the child demanded. Bess glanced at her purse, and in seconds, the little girl had found the nitroglycerin, opened the childproof cap, and placed a pill gently in Bess's mouth. Bess rolled it under her tongue, and closed her eyes. The pain was so harsh.

"Take two," the little voice commanded, and Bess complied, smiling despite the pressure in her chest. Gradually the pain retreated.

"Mom! What happened?" shouted Bess's son, Dan, as he pushed through the crowd.

"Zosia!" screeched a voice, and a red-haired woman rushed up to the little girl and hugged her tightly. She said something to the child in a language Bess didn't understand.

The nitro had done its work, and Bess kissed her son. "Just an angina attack. I haven't had one for so long I forgot how bad they can be."

Bess didn't argue when Dan suggested they stop at the hospital on the way home. The pain had never been so strong before. Then she turned to the little girl, who still held her hand.

"Thank you, sweetheart," Bess said, giving the little hand a gentle squeeze. "For such a little angel, you're very smart and brave!"

"Excuse me, I'm Zosia's aunt," said the woman, who spoke with a slight accent. "I don't know how Zosia ended up over here—we just stepped off a plane from Poland. But thank you for your kind words." She spoke rapidly to the child in Polish. Zosia chattered back in the same language and smiled shyly at Bess.

"Zosia says she's happy you're better," said the girl's aunt.

"But, why doesn't *she* say it?" Bess asked, surprised.

"She can't. Zosia doesn't know English yet!" said the woman laughing, as they waved gaily and disappeared into the crowd.

PRIORITIES

I did not do my work today,
The dishes sit in the sink.
The laundry is dirty, the trash isn't out—
Oh, what will the neighbors think?
I did not do my work today,
I didn't even make the bed,
But gathered together my little ones dear,
And danced with the angels instead.

Maker of us all, help us to appreciate the
gifts of children: those we see daily, those
who live across the globe, and those
whose angelic spirits touch us from
another time.

It is said, and it is true, that just before we are born [an] angel puts his finger to our lips and says, "Hush, don't tell what you know." This is why we are born with a cleft on our upper lips and remembering nothing of where we came from."

RODERICK MACLEISH, PRINCE OMBRA

THE WISE AND THE WHYS

"Mommy, why do we have blessings?" Kaitlyn drew a wide arch with the fat yellow marking pen clutched in her hand. Then she recapped the pen and reached for a purple one. "Why?" she asked again.

"Because that's how God shows he loves us."

"Why?"

Sue sighed. "You know how Mommy and Daddy like to surprise you for your birthday? Well, blessings are like that. God's surprises."

"Mommy, why don't we look for the surprises?" said Kaitlyn as she added a swipe of green.

Yes, why don't we? Sue thought. Her mind drifted to the demands of work and parenting, the hustle of different schedules. She often forgot to search for blessings. What were they? And where exactly were they?

Sue glanced at the drawing her four-year-old placed in her hands. A bright, arcing rainbow!

"You know, Kaitlyn, blessings are where you find them. Just like rainbows. And, besides, young lady, just why is it you are so full of questions about blessings?"

"Because," her dimpled cheeks rounded into a smile, "yesterday I surprised Grammy. I picked all the pretty pink flowers in her yard. She said, 'Oh, well, maybe they'd be prettier inside, anyway, in a vase where we can look at them.' And then Grammy hugged me and said *I* was her *most* precious blessing!"

A smile of pure joy curved Sue's lips. Sometimes, she thought, it takes an angel to ask the question that points us to the answer.

Focus on a four-year-old, whatever disposition, and somewhere in there you'll find an angel.

⊱⊶⊙⊷⊰

We are blessed by your sending your littlest angels, Lord. Their small wings take us beyond disillusionment. Their tilted haloes remind us that you have set them apart to do wonderful things in their lives and in ours.

⊱⊶⊙⊷⊰

WHERE DID YOU COME FROM?

Where did you come from, baby dear?
Out of the everywhere into here.
Where did you get your eyes so blue?
Out of the sky as I came through.
What makes the light in them sparkle
      and spin?
Some of the starry spikes left in.
Where did you get that little tear?
I found it waiting when I got here.

What makes your forehead so smooth
    and high?
A soft hand stroked it as I went by,
What makes your cheek like a warm white
    rose?
I saw something better than anyone
    knows.
Whence that three-corner'd smile of bliss?
Three angels gave me at once a kiss.
Where did you get this pearly ear?
God spoke, and it came out to hear.

Where did you get those arms and hands?
Love made itself into hooks and bands.
Whence did you come, you darling things?
From the same box as the cherubs' wings.
Where did you get that dimple so cute,
God touched my cheek as I came through.
How did they all just come to be you?
God thought of me, and so I grew.
But how did you come to us, you dear?
God thought of you, and so I am here.

GEORGE MACDONALD, 1871

*Little angel baby, so recently come to
earth,
What do you remember from your life
before your birth?
There must be a reason why you smile at
the ceiling above:
Your angel friends are visiting and
whispering their love.*

LOST MOTHER

At age 19, Melanie was already divorced and had a one-year-old child. Her mother was happy to let Melanie and her daughter move back home but reminded her she would have to help with expenses. So Melanie found a job as a cocktail waitress at a club on the outskirts of town.

There she met Skip, a man who told her he loved her and that she was being wasted in a one-horse town. He talked of places that never went to sleep, where neon lights turned the night into perpetual sunrise and money was to be made with a roll of the dice. He begged her to come with him to Las Vegas.

She naively believed Skip when he said they should go first without the baby and come back for her once they were settled. Melanie was not sure she should leave little Kari, but she was young and in love. If she let this chance for happiness go by, she would regret it for the rest of her life. Leaving Kari with loving grandparents made it easier to say goodbye...or would have, except for her mother's stony look and stern warning that something was "not right" about Skip.

Her mother's words faded in Melanie's memory, because when they got to Las Vegas, Skip was wonderful. He bought her beautiful clothes, paid for her to be pampered in a beauty salon, and squired her all over town to dinners, clubs, shows, and casinos. He walked proudly with her on his arm, and she had never felt so beautiful and loved. Then, a few weeks later, he asked her to have dinner alone with a client to help close a deal he was working on. She felt like she'd been punched in the stomach. He promised it would only be this one time— he'd be forever in her debt, he confided softly, and hinted that afterward they would get married. Horrified, Melanie refused. She suddenly realized her mother might have been right. She missed her mother and felt so alone. Yet this was the man she loved, and despite this insane request, she believed he loved her, too.

Skip continued to be affectionate, but he never did propose marriage. After several weeks she realized he had other women. Melanie was so depressed and embarrassed by the situation she'd gotten herself into that she avoided all contact with her parents and daughter. It would be better if I was dead, she began to think.

One evening, as Melanie waited morosely in a hotel lobby for Skip, a little girl walked up to her, crying, "My mommy is lost!" Melanie reached out to comfort the child, but suddenly she saw her own daughter crying and saying it, too: "My mommy is lost," over and over. As Melanie hugged the crying child, a voice inside her head cried out, *What am I doing here? Why am I so lost?* She helped the little girl find her frantic parents and could hardly swallow for the lump in her throat as she watched them embrace. Then she walked briskly out of the hotel and caught a cab for the airport, where she booked the first flight home to her own little girl. While she waited for her flight, she thought how miraculous it was that the lost little girl had chosen to come up to her at the hotel when there were several other women present. She must have been an angel, Melanie thought, who helps lost mothers find themselves.

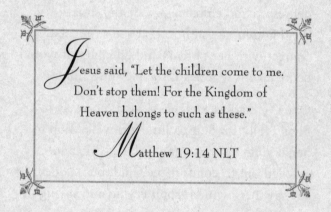

Jesus said, "Let the children come to me. Don't stop them! For the Kingdom of Heaven belongs to such as these."

Matthew 19:14 NLT

Thank you for these little hands that hold to mine and give me peace. Thank you for these open minds who rescue me from forgetting that the world is full of hope. Thank you for these little angels who bring me a tad of heaven with every smile so I can believe again.

ALL DIRECTIONS

You come at me from all directions,
You swoop, you run, you play,
You must be angels with heavenly wings,
To dance around this way.
You come at me from all directions,
Some days I'm wearing thin,
But love flies in, too, with the breeze,
So swoop at me again.

BEST INTENTIONS

Babies are truly angels sent from heaven. One has only to look at their little cheeks, their big eyes, their innocent faces to realize it. Sometimes they arrive at what seems like the most inopportune time, and other times they fail to manifest, even when they are fervently wanted. For many women, there is nothing quite like a baby to bring happiness. Cathy and Rachel were such women, an unlikely pair brought together by the sudden appearance of one particular little bundle of joy.

Cathy was actually little more than a child herself, still immersed in the game of rebelling against her parents, when she became a parent. Because it was an embarrassment to the family, they sent Cathy to a small town in the country to live with her Aunt Rachel, a sweet woman whose one regret in life was that she could never have children.

Cathy felt abandoned by her parents and boyfriend. Fiercely, she vowed she would never abandon the babe in her arms. It occurred to her that it was unjust that a baby would be born to a careless teenager like herself, who had not even wanted one, when sweet Aunt Rachel would have given her right arm for such a chance. Raising this child would take a good 18 years—another entire lifetime. Cathy knew she wasn't ready for this, but she was willing to do her best.

Rachel, too, couldn't help wondering why this angel baby was bestowed upon a wild 17-year-old, when she, who'd prayed desperately for so many years, had been denied. Yet as she watched Cathy hug her chubby infant son, Rachel acknowledged that God must have his reasons. She resolved to embrace Cathy and the baby without further questioning God's intent.

Helping Cathy diaper her infant son, Rachel smiled her most gentle smile. "I do believe," she said, with a twinkle in her eye, "we're turning out to be our very own happy little family."

You came into my life,
Down from heaven above,
Someone I could care for,
Someone I could love.
God's newest creation,
Perfect in my eyes,
My darling little baby—
My angel in disguise.

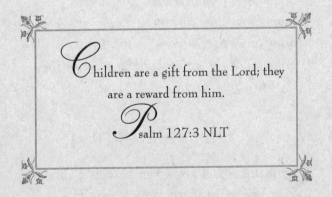

Children are a gift from the Lord; they are a reward from him.

Psalm 127:3 NLT

*Gracious God, help us to learn from the
children in our lives. Let us view the
world with their innocent eyes and laugh
joyously with them at the wonder of your
creation. Make us mindful of others' hurts
and sympathetic to others' needs.
Open our hearts to the world, as children
open themselves, with delight and
curiosity, to all the world's experiences.*

SLEEPING ANGELS

*I find sleeping angels all around my house:
Sometimes they're on my bed,
Sometimes on the couch.
Sometimes they curl up in a pile,
Sometimes they snooze by the TV,
Sometimes I'm either holding them or they
    are holding me.*

SHEAR DELIGHT

Stephanie was a giver. Her parents claimed
she was born sharing. As a baby, she
offered her pacifier to big brother Caleb. Once

she sent her doll home with a playmate who didn't have one. For her sixth birthday, instead of birthday gifts she asked her friends to donate shampoos and soaps to a homeless shelter. When she turned seven, Stephanie read a newspaper article requesting bicycles for needy children, and she donated hers.

Now she was nearly eight and, in her words, "mostly grown up."

One morning she announced, "Mother, I thought about it all night. I want to celebrate my birthday this month by getting my first haircut."

"But, Stephanie, you love your long hair. Why do you want to cut it?"

"I want to give it away...well, half of it anyway."

Her mother's eyebrows shot up. "Give it away?"

"I saw a TV show last night about a place that makes wigs." Stephanie's concern showed in her furrowed brow. "Did you know some kids are bald? They have diseases that make them lose their hair." She looked up at her mother with troubled eyes. "I bet they get teased. I bet they *hate* looking different."

Stephanie fanned out her shiny hair. "You've always said I had enough hair for three girls. Do you suppose they could really get three wigs from it?"

After a long silence, her mother stooped to press her face into her daughter's long, dark hair. "I'm sure they could make at least one."

"Only one?" She couldn't hide her disappointment. Then her dimpled smile returned. "Just think, one less kid will feel different."

Her mother made the necessary arrangements, and a few days later they were at the hair salon. Stephanie hesitated only a minute before climbing into the chair.

"Stephanie..."

"Don't worry, Mother. I'm sure."

The hairstylist combed the girl's tumbling hair and wrapped it in an elastic band. Then she braided it from below Stephanie's shoulders to her hips. She tied off the thick end of the long braid with another band, then held up the sharp shears.

"Ready?"

"Ready." Stephanie scrunched her eyes closed and held her breath.

Snip, snip. Snip, snip, snip. It was done.

Stephanie's eyes danced when she saw the newly cut braid.

"Let's measure it," the stylist suggested. "Wow! It's 16 inches. The kids will love getting this!' Then she picked up the scissors and said, "Now, let's trim you up."

Afterward, Stephanie tossed her head, testing her new look. "My head feels lighter," she reported.

"So does my heart. What a special gift you're giving," said the stylist, handing her the braid in a plastic bag. "Well, Stephanie, now what?"

Stephanie didn't even hesitate. "Now I'll see how fast I can grow it again. I really want to make another kid happy!"

LITTLE ANGEL

You see a world, little angel,
That I forgot about long ago.
You make me believe,
You help me to see
What a little faith will do.

You see a world, little angel,
That I may have given up on,
Many tears ago,
Many years ago,
Were it not for love and you.

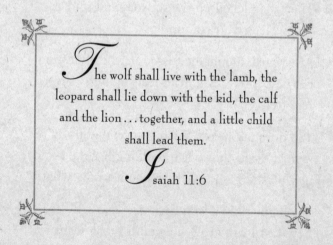

The wolf shall live with the lamb, the leopard shall lie down with the kid, the calf and the lion . . . together, and a little child shall lead them.

Isaiah 11:6

~ *Chapter Three* ~

ANGELS IN UNIFORM

May the Babe of Bethlehem be yours to tend;
May the Boy of Nazareth be yours for friend;
May the Man of Galilee his healing send;
May the Christ of Calvary his courage lend;
May the Risen Lord his presence send;
And his holy angels defend you to the end.

"PILGRIM'S PRAYER," FOUND IN
OBERAMMERGAU, GERMANY

⋗—⟨⋗—○—⟨⋗—⟨

The angels . . . regard our safety, undertake our
defense, direct our ways and exercise a constant
solicitude that no evil befalls us.

JOHN CALVIN, INSTITUTES OF THE
CHRISTIAN RELIGION, BOOK 1

SILVER-HAIRED ANGEL

It was 2:00 A.M. Jean sat by her husband Joe's bed in the Critical Care Unit of the small rural hospital. *This nightmare can't be happening,* Jean thought. She felt helpless; she knew Joe's infection continued to rage, and the doctors weren't even sure what was causing it to spread.

There were only a few patients in the unit, the earlier intense activity had quieted, and the lights had been dimmed. Two nurses sat at a station in the center of a small suite of rooms keeping tabs on the array of monitors. Jean closed her eyes and pleaded with the universe to spare Joe. When she opened her eyes again, a nurse was walking into the darkened room. The nurse stopped by Joe's bed and looked intently at Jean. When the nurse spoke, her voice was soft but urgent.

"We think we have figured out what's causing the infection to spread. A resilient bacteria has been detected in Joe's latest blood culture. The only effective means that we know can eradicate this bacteria is a new medication.

With your permission, the doctor would like to start the medication immediately. Is this okay with you?"

Jean nodded. Joe groaned in his sleep, and Jean bent over him to comfort him. When she looked up, the nurse was gone. *She's gone to get the new medicine,* Jean thought gratefully. She stepped to the door and glanced over at the nurses' station. The two nurses were still seated, chatting and watching the monitors, as if nothing had changed.

"Excuse me," Jean said, striding over, "did the other nurse go to get the new medicine?"

"I don't know what you're talking about," said one of the nurses. "We're the only ones here, and we haven't gotten any new orders for your husband."

"But the older nurse, the one with the silver hair...." Jean trailed off. Her words were met with blank stares.

Jean said anxiously, "She was just here. She said the new medicine had to be started immediately."

"I'm sorry," the other nurse began, "the doctor was called to the emergency room an hour ago, and no one has been in here recently except us. We don't have any new orders."

Then, seeing that Jean was near hysteria, she offered, "Why don't I contact the doctor for you." She pushed a few buttons on the telephone, "Hello. This is Susan from the Critical Care Unit. I was calling about.... Yes. Yes. Certainly. We'll start it right away."

The nurse furrowed her brow as she looked at Jean, "I don't know how you knew all this; the doctor just learned it himself. But you were right." She grabbed some keys and walked quickly to the medicine closet as the other nurse escorted Jean back to Joe's room.

The next morning Jean was dozing in the chair by Joe's bed. She was still holding his hand from the night before. Joe shook her hand gently and groggily said, "Hey, honey, wake up. Do they serve breakfast in this place?"

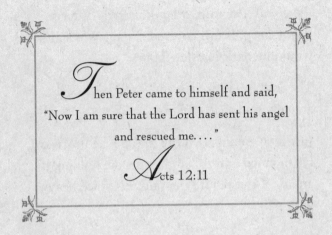

*T*hen Peter came to himself and said, "Now I am sure that the Lord has sent his angel and rescued me. . . ."

*A*cts 12:11

A Troop of Smiling Angels

"*Y*ou said there would be water along the trail," Grace accused Adam.

"I didn't realize those squiggly lines on the map meant the stream was 300 feet down! You'll be fine. We have water back at the car."

Grace suspected they were also lost, but she didn't know how to read a topographical map either. It was late August, and they'd been hiking along this narrow ridge in Virginia's Blue Ridge Mountains for hours without water. They'd finished the little they'd brought, but if there was a stream, it lay hundreds of feet down steep, brush-covered slopes. Worse, it would be dark in a few hours.

The trail began to descend—maybe they'd actually find that stream.

Just then Adam cried out and pitched forward. He moaned and rolled on his side, holding his ankle. "I twisted it," he said, his voice heavy with pain.

Grace felt sorry for Adam, but she was also angry that he'd let his overconfidence get them in this fix. "What now?"

"I don't know. I'm not sure I can walk," Adam grunted, sitting back against a tree. "I'm really sorry, Grace."

She tried to smile. "You rest. I'll check on ahead."

Over Adam's weak objections, Grace started down the trail. Her muscles complained, and the new hiking boots rubbed her heels. As she walked, the sun settled behind the trees, and suddenly she shivered. She paused, wondering if she should go back.

But...was that singing? It came from somewhere to her right. A small path twisted off the main trail through boulders and trees, and Grace decided to follow it. As she rounded a stand of pine trees, she stopped, wondering if she was hallucinating. There was a shelter, tents, and lots of teenage girls, all in matching shirts.

"Hi," they called when they saw Grace.

They were scouts! When they learned of Grace and Adam's predicament, the troop leader and several older girls grabbed flashlights and packs and started up the trail for Adam, while the rest gathered around Grace, who was savoring the refreshing water. They brought a map and explained their location: near a stream, but far from any roads.

"Don't worry," one scout said, "you can stay tonight with us, and we'll get you out tomorrow."

Through a mist of gratitude and relief, Grace grinned at the troop of smiling angels.

Watchful God,
Thank you for those persons in uniform
who have watched over us and cared for
us. Bless them, guide them in their duties,
and keep them safe.

⊱━◦━⊰

But if these beings guard you, they do so
because they have been summoned by
your prayers.

SAINT AMBROSE

MORGAN'S DOLL

Having recently signed up as a Red Cross volunteer, Katie called the state headquarters and was directed to go to a town ten miles east to help assess the tornado's damage and direct people to the local shelter. When she arrived, she was shocked. There were no houses, no trees, no cars parked in driveways. Only devastation and debris piled high.

Katie's eyes fell upon a little girl standing with her family. She was maybe five or six, and the pain and terror in her eyes made Katie's heart break.

The little girl's name was Morgan, and her family, the Murphys, had lived in their house for more than 20 years. As Katie led them toward a van that would take them to a local shelter at a nearby elementary school, Morgan, crying, broke away and ran back toward the rubble that had once been her home. Mrs. Murphy and Katie ran back to get Morgan. Mrs. Murphy spoke softly to her little girl, urging her to come with them and forget "Ellie."

Katie bent down and asked, "How are you doing, Morgan?" Morgan just nodded, as if to say okay, and whispered, "But what about Ellie?" Katie sat down next to Morgan and asked her what Ellie looked like. Morgan's eyes lit as she described a big cloth doll with brown braids and a freckled nose.

"I'm sure you will see Ellie again soon," was all Katie could think of to say. But Morgan just looked down and said, "Ellie's gone forever." Katie then knew what she had to do. No matter how many people she helped that night, it just wouldn't be enough unless she could make this little girl smile again.

After seeing the family off in the van, Katie walked back to where the Murphys' home had once stood. She knew there was little chance of finding Ellie, but she also knew that if she didn't try she would never forgive herself.

She put on a pair of thick work gloves and began the slow, tedious effort of looking for a needle in a haystack. After digging for a while, Katie was startled when a male voice behind her boomed, "What are you doing here?" She turned to face a tall, muscular police officer who was glaring at her suspiciously. His badge read "Dan." He informed her that she was trespassing and demanded that she leave.

Then Katie decided to tell the officer about Morgan. To Katie's surprise, Dan offered his help. He got in his patrol car, positioned it toward the rubble, and turned on the high beams. In that light, they searched together for Morgan's doll.

After several hours, the helpful officer had to leave to check on a looting incident a few streets away. He told Katie he would be back, but she told him not to bother, that she would probably be gone by then.

As Dan drove away, Katie told herself she would stay one more hour. An hour later, she called it quits.

The next morning, Katie went to visit the Murphys at the shelter. She sat next to Morgan and was about to make up some story about Ellie that she hoped would comfort Morgan when a hand squeezed her shoulder. She looked up to see Dan standing over them. He was holding something in his other hand, and he held it toward them. "Ellie!" Morgan shouted over and over again.

Morgan took her beloved doll and held it tight, and her family held each other. Katie could see the hope in their eyes, and she knew this was the beginning of a journey to healing. For Morgan, that healing would be a bit easier with her faithful companion.

*Lord, remind us of a childhood memory
of someone in uniform who made a
difference in our lives. A school nurse who
comforted us, a firefighter who spoke to
us on a field trip to the local station, a
police officer standing on a neighborhood
corner, a doctor who treated us for a
childhood illness. Thank you for showing
us that someone in uniform could be
trusted and could be a friend.*

<hr />

*We cannot part with our friends; we
cannot let our angels go.*

RALPH WALDO EMERSON, "COMPENSATION"

<hr />

*May we see those who work among us for
who they truly are:
Angels without wings,
Blessing our lives with the most
 extraordinary things.*

ON ELEPHANTS AND ANGELS

Martha's grandmother held that everyone would encounter an angel in disguise at least once in their lifetime. Martha's came in the being of a 19-year-old woman dressed in a hospital housekeeper's uniform. Her name was Patricia.

Martha was age 22 when she met Patricia. Seemingly healthy except for some swelling and a few pesky sores on her legs, Martha was hospitalized for tests. It took four months for the doctors to diagnose an inflammation of Martha's blood vessels caused by systemic lupus. Her right leg was amputated, and she was left with nerve damage and deformity of her left leg and foot. Worse yet, as far as her vanity was concerned, steroids had distorted her facial features and inflated her body shape. The crowning blow was the loss of her hair from aggressive chemotherapy. Martha had stopped looking in the mirror.

Only Patricia seemed oblivious to the ravages of Martha's illness. Other visitors averted their eyes. Even nurses seemed to look anywhere but at Martha. The clinking of Patricia's massive key ring announced her arrival each morning. She'd walk straight to Martha's bed and look directly at her. "Hello. Are you better today?"

Patricia asked the question with such utter sincerity and hope that Martha felt obligated to answer "a little better," even on her worst days. Patricia would then set about her tasks. While she worked, she shared stories about her family and her pet cat, Boo.

One morning, during Patricia's regular visiting time, Martha was on a stretcher in the hallway waiting for a ride to the operating room for a bone graft. She felt despondent and full of self-pity. A tear trickled down her cheek. As she wiped the tear away, she felt a tap on her shoulder. There stood Patricia, her face full of love and concern. She pressed something in Martha's hand.

"You hold it," Patricia said. "It always gives me the best luck." She had placed a blue plastic elephant in Martha's hand; it had always hung on Patricia's key ring.

Patricia said, "It's blue, just like your eyes."

Martha smiled. Through all her deformities, Patricia saw the one part of Martha that had not changed: her eyes. Martha realized Patricia loved her the way God did—unconditionally.

"Thanks, Patricia," Martha said. "I'll take good care of it."

The blue elephant saw Martha through the surgery, then months of physical therapy and rehabilitation. Once in a while, Patricia would stop by Martha's new room on her way home and visit for a few minutes before she had to leave. She always had a funny story to tell about Boo's latest feline escapades.

When the morning of Martha's discharge finally arrived, Patricia was right there. Patricia insisted Martha keep the elephant. "So you'll remember me," she added.

Martha gave her a big hug. "I'll always remember you, Patricia."

Patricia grinned. "You're my friend. I'll remember you, too."

Over the next few years, Martha sent notes and cards to Patricia through the housekeeping department of the hospital. Then one day Martha's letter was returned. Patricia no longer worked there, and she had left no forwarding address. But Martha still has contact with Patricia through the little blue elephant that sits on her mantel. No other gift could compare to this treasured gift of unconditional love from an angel in disguise.

God, bless those angels who shake hands with danger on a daily basis. Help them to know that their efforts are not only noticed but appreciated. Give them courage with caution. Give them life with meaning. Give them the strength to withstand the pressure and risk.

ANGELIC FIREFIGHTERS

Arriving in red chariots, they fly into leaping embers and raging infernos until they save the frightened and deliver feathered kisses in the form of smudged fingerprints of love.

LONG MAY IT WAVE

Morning sun glinted on Doug's carroty hair as he tightened the eagle slide that anchored his Boy Scout neckerchief. He gazed out from his vantage point onstage, observing the families that blanketed the tender June grass on the hillside facing the amphitheater. Behind him, the 101st Colorado Army National Guard Band tuned its instruments, as discordant as the honking geese dotting the pond across the way. The high-school JROTC stood to the side in formation.

This was it, the Flag Day ceremony that culminated Doug's yearlong Eagle Scout Project.

Born on November 11, the freckle-faced 14-year-old had a special affinity for patriotism. His early birthday parties centered around flag-raisings and attending the annual Veterans Day parade where he admired the long strides of uniformed soldiers. Doug grinned, remembering that when he was five he had assumed the parade was in his honor. At a tender age, he studied flag history, symbolism, and etiquette. It seemed only natural to make

The Stars and Stripes the nucleus of his Eagle Scout service project.

The project itself wasn't unique. Doug knew it had been done locally once before, a long time before. A look around town made it obvious that it needed to be organized again. So he set in motion his plan: collecting bedraggled American flags for proper disposal.

But the scope and impact of the project surprised even him. Area newspapers caught the spirit and promoted the event. Their focused publicity brought phone call after phone call from people with frayed and faded flags. Surprisingly, most of the requests came from retired veterans and others with a military connection. Doug organized his Boy Scout troop to collect the battered banners. They didn't realize they would also collect stirring stories.

One eager vet who had served in Korea invited them into his garage. From a high shelf, he reverently handed the boys four flags, dusty from storage, tattered with use. Each was still perfectly, properly folded in a trim triangle with only the blue field showing.

From his couch, a disabled World War II veteran waved the scouts inside his home. Watery gray eyes focused somewhere beyond them while he dredged up nearly forgotten battle memories. "I've been waiting to get rid of this old flag, boys. Just wanted to do it proper-like." He pressed a ragged triangle into Doug's hands.

Contacted for assistance, local service clubs donated crisp, new flags for people requesting replacements. As the scouts lowered a survivor's faded flag and raised a pristine Stars and Stripes, the veteran shed tears in remembrance of the buddy he had lost in the Persian Gulf.

Another day, a gray-haired mother met them at her door. Her flag was oversized, spotless, like new. Seeing their questioning eyes, she explained, "This flag covered my Joey's casket. He died in Vietnam during his second tour of duty. It's time to discard it—along with the stigma."

So it went. After hearing many of these stories, Doug began to realize that it wasn't so much about the actual flag, but about the people who believed in the flag and who were willing to fight and die for it. It was then he decided to alter his project, not simply to dispose of each flag with dignity, but to collect each story that went with that flag. To let the flag go, but to make sure the story lived on.

So as the band played the last strains of "The Star-Spangled Banner," the first speaker came up to tell the audience the story of his flag and its angels.

Father God, thank you for those angelic persons who bring healing. We will try to mimic their ways.

Who does the best his circumstance allows does well, acts nobly; angels could do no more.

EDWARD YOUNG, NIGHT THOUGHTS

But we appeal to you, brothers and sisters, to respect those who labor among you, and have charge of you in the Lord and admonish you; esteem them very highly in love because of their work.

1 Thessalonians 5:12–13

MESSENGER ANGELS

*Angels are spirits, but it is not because they are
spirits that they are angels. They become angels
when they are sent. For the name angel refers to
their office, not their nature. You ask the name
of this nature, it is spirit; you ask its office, it is
that of an Angel, which is a messenger.*

ST. AUGUSTINE

>—<>—o—<>—<

*Creator of all that exists, come to me
as you came to so many—in the guise
of angels. Speak to me your message.
Open my ears that I might hear your
words. And give me understanding of
what you would have me do.*

LIBRARY OF LOVE

Jerry was embarrassed when he got home and realized that he still had the book Laura had given him to read. That New Year's Day had been tough, and he almost hadn't accepted the invitation to spend it at the home of his out-of-town friends, Laura and Tom.

Having lost first his wife, Kathy, and then his job in recent months, Jerry had felt almost too down to present a "game face" to his old friends. Yet something urged him to go. When he arrived, he smelled Laura's vegetable beef soup simmering on the stove. His friends' two young boys jumped up on him like puppies, begging to wrestle with "Uncle Jerry." He began to relax, relieved that no one was going to mention Kathy unless he did, nor ask him how he was doing in his job search.

Following a long tromp in the woods after lunch, Jerry exchanged Christmas gifts with Laura and Tom's family, just as they'd done when Kathy was alive. The ritual felt empty without Kathy's gifts, carefully chosen and beautifully wrapped. Afterward, Laura casually picked up a book that had been lying on the table and handed it to Jerry. "I wonder if you might like this," she said. "Someone gave it to me. I'm partway through." Jerry halfheartedly flipped through the book; self-help books were not for him.

When he returned home and unpacked, Jerry discovered the book in the box with the flannel shirt his friends had given him. Because the next day was Sunday and he couldn't mail the book back to Laura then, he found himself reading it. What struck him most was a passage that described fear as natural. Like all other emotions, whether joyous or painful, the book said fear will pass.

Jerry suddenly knew that what had been bothering him so much was not his grief for Kathy nor his humiliation and worry about having lost his job but fear. Fear that he would always feel as sad about Kathy as he did now, fear that he would not find another job, fear that he would lose his home. He realized he had been bracing himself for the new year as if he had been sitting in the dentist's chair. The book's message helped him recognize that fear is normal, but he was still afraid. However, instead of fighting the fear as an enemy, he greeted it as an old acquaintance that he didn't like but would have to spend some time with. He was no longer afraid of being afraid.

After finishing the book, he called Laura to say how sorry he was that he had accidentally taken it home. Laura told him that the friend who had given it to her had found it helpful while recovering from breast cancer and that, in fact, what she had read so far had helped her with a recent bout of depression. Jerry would never have guessed that; Laura was always serene and smiling. He assured her that he would put it in the mail so she could finish reading it. "No rush," Laura said. "Books have a habit of finding their way into the hands of those who need them most."

*In the Bible, angels appeared to a variety
of people with messages appropriate to the
person and situation. If an angel were to
come to you today, what message do you
think you would receive?*

    You are truly blessed!

    The Lord is with you.

    Don't be afraid!

CHARMED

Sonya donned the gauzy, satin-edged veil
then turned to look into the cheval mirror.
A dry-eyed vision in white gazed steadfastly
back. This wasn't the wedding of her little-girl
dreams. There was no mother to help tame her
tumbling curls. No mother to fasten the 22
hand-covered buttons down the back of her
gown. No mother to lift and settle the yards of
rich, embroidered satin. No mother to share
her wedding day.

The emptiness she felt wasn't new. Her mother
had died 15 years earlier and with her died
many of Sonya's dreams. She shook her head
and sighed. Shouldn't she be accustomed to

doing things for herself, by herself? She'd had years of practice. Well, not exactly by herself, she admitted. Her dad had been there for her. A slight chuckle tilted the corners of her mouth. The two of them had survived Sonya's awkward preteen years and then her full-blown plunge into adolescence—makeup, nylons, dating. Her dad had seen her through it all. But, in their hearts, both of them knew how much smoother the voyage would have been with her mother helping to steer the way. For the first time in a long time, Sonya felt her mother's absence deeply. Never had she felt more alone, profoundly alone.

With one final, satisfied glance at her reflection, Sonya turned away to answer a soft knock at the door. Standing in the doorway, her dad caught his breath when he saw his daughter. His eyes softened and he said, "You're beautiful, sweetheart, beautiful. You look exactly like your mother. Especially wearing her gown." After a long pause, he cleared his throat. Sweeping her into a hug, he held her close and then at arm's length to admire her once more.

"I know you miss your mother, Sonya. Especially now. That's why I chose today to give you the bracelet she wore at our wedding ceremony." Her dad reached into his pocket and brought out a delicate silver chain. He fumbled to secure the clasp at her wrist while Sonya held back her tears. Her father gently flicked the charm dangling from the chain. "You know, it's funny." He said, "I could've sworn your mother had only a chain. I was surprised when I got it from your mother's jewelry box last night. For the life of me, I don't remember adding a charm to her bracelet. She must have added it herself!"

"Oh, Dad, look closely." A sob escaped. "It's an angel!" Entranced, Sonya turned her wrist to admire the gold charm. Her dad smiled, kissed her cheek, and left, closing the door quietly behind him.

Sonya turned and walked back to the mirror. Through a mist of tulle and tears, she knew her mother's love was with her after all on her wedding day.

Around our pillow golden ladders rise
And up and down the skies
With winged sandals shod
The Angels come and go,
The Messengers of God.

R.H. STODDARD

REAL-LIFE DRAMA

Tasha and Claire had been inseparable friends in high school, but now, two years after graduation, they had grown apart. Tasha had gone to New York to study theater; Claire had stayed in the Midwest, living at an inner-city house that ministered to the poor, where she was a full-time volunteer.

Gradually their e-mails had become less frequent. They reconnected, however, when Tasha was home on Christmas break. Claire called and asked if Tasha might like to see a play about her heroine, the late Dorothy Day. Day was the cofounder of the Catholic Worker movement, which believes in the God-given dignity of every human being, and the workers try to see this in all whom they encounter.

Tasha, being accustomed to Broadway theater, didn't have high expectations of this play, but she did want to see Claire. On a frigid night when the sky was pewter gray, she picked up Claire in the rundown neighborhood where she lived. As they were leaving, Claire noticed a solitary silhouette slumped on the porch. "Oh, Teddy!" she cried. She explained to Tasha that Teddy was an alcoholic and a diabetic with a host of problems, the most recent of which was severely infected feet. He refused to go to a doctor, so Claire did what she could. The young women had no choice but to go back into the house and tend to him. Tasha sighed, thinking *typical Claire.* In Tasha's view, there was no point in going to a play if you missed the beginning, and besides it was rude to arrive late.

Once inside the house, it became obvious that Teddy reeked, but Claire merely teased him, holding her nose and shaking her head. Tasha watched her friend's deft fingers patiently go about the job of washing and bandaging his feet and ankles, gently asking him where he was sleeping and if he had enough to eat.

After he shuffled away, the two friends slipped out, getting to the theater in time for the second act. During one scene, the Dorothy Day character reluctantly allows a desperately poor woman to sleep in her apartment, thus launching the enduring international Houses of Hospitality like the one where Claire now lived. Forced to practice what she preached, the Day character turned to the audience and said, "It is a fearful thing to look into the face of the living God."

Hearing those words reminded Tasha that there is wisdom that goes far beyond theater etiquette.

God, bless the angels of our world that call us to a better life. Whoever they may be, keep them strong. Give them a sense of their message and influence. Humble them with the reality of the power they wield in the lives of those around them. Bless these angels, Lord. Make them strong.

SMILEY GIRL

Once again, Bess couldn't sleep. She lay awake, feeling miserable. Was she sick? No, it was just nerves. But why couldn't she sleep? She wasn't the nervous type. Her father, who had passed on 20 years ago, used to call her "Smiley Girl," so what in the world could have made her feel so anxious?

Part of it, she knew, was her job. After 15 years, Bess didn't know if she was up to it anymore. More and more, things in the accounting department were automated, but it seemed to take forever to get the new systems working right. Meanwhile, she had to bear the brunt of customers unhappy with mistakes on their bills, with suppliers angry because they'd been paid too little, and today the rotten computer kept freezing up, right in the middle of payroll! Bess had blown up, and then sat there feeling foolish and helpless while a nice computer whiz came and hunched over the keyboard, and—poof!—things were fixed . . . until the next day.

Another source of anxiety was her daughter, Karen. She had always been a moody girl, but after a year at college, she had moved back home and declared she was taking a year off to get a job. Everyone loved Karen, but her abrupt return had upset the delicate equilibrium of the household. Since she'd been back, Karen always seemed to be fighting with someone: her mom, her sister, her father. The worst part was that Bess felt powerless to help any of them.

There also was Jeff, Bess's husband, who was always tense, nervous, and absent from home. But Bess couldn't complain because, after all, this had only started after he quit his job to open his own consulting company. She felt guilty for feeling so angry. As Jeff often reminded her: "Honey, I'm doing this for our future!"

But, as far as Bess could see, her future loomed empty and bleak. Bess wasn't even sure she wanted to go there, but the alternative...she drifted off to sleep. She began to dream and heard the sound of her father's footsteps in the hall growing louder. Bess sat up in bed, staring into the dark hall.

"Daddy?" she said. Then, as clearly as if one of her children was standing there, she saw her dad's face. He smiled, a broad, beatific smile and said, *Hang in there, Smiley Girl, everything's gonna be okay. You get on to sleep now.*

Then he started to walk away. "Daddy, wait!" she cried. *Relax now, sweetheart. You're doing just fine. Everyone has to make their own way, and things will find a way to work out. Don't forget how much I love you.*

Bess watched him return to the hallway. She didn't try to run after him. Bess woke up from her dream, feeling calm and, most of all, loved. She knew her dad was right: Everything would be okay, even if things weren't easy. She lay back on the pillow, relaxing into the wonderful feeling of peace and calm. Then, for the first time in a long while, Bess remembered that, truly, she could handle just about anything. "Dad," she whispered, "thanks so much." Then she fell asleep.

Here I stand at a crossroads,
Wondering which way I should go.
I ask for a sign, but in my heart,
I believe I already know.
Intuition, inspiration?
No. My angel told me so.

MESSAGE RECEIVED

Maggie sat in the waiting room...waiting. She'd spent a lot of time there this past week. So much time that she knew the room's contents by heart: *Cosmopolitan* magazine with its seductive cover torn in half. Plum-colored chair with the sagging seat. Jumble of newspapers mixed with dog-eared medical brochures. It looked like she would be here for several more days. Her husband's heart-bypass surgery had been a gift until the complications set in. Now his condition was more critical than ever.

Oh, Rick, just keep fighting, she prayed. *Please, God, help him live.*

"Excuse me. Haven't I seen you here before?"

Maggie opened her eyes and focused on the attractive, silver-haired volunteer seating herself nearby.

"My name is Betty."

"Maggie. I'm Maggie." *And I'm in no mood for idle chitchat.*

"Is your husband in ICU?"

"Yes."

"I can tell by the strain in your face and voice that you've been here a long time."

Maggie softened at the woman's intuitiveness. "Yes. All this waiting is pretty hard."

Betty reached over and gave her arm a grandmotherly pat.

"Well, dear, what can I do to make it easier? Something to read? Should I turn on the television?"

"Nothing, thank you. I can't seem to focus."

"How do you relax at home? What eases your tension, frees your mind?"

Maggie thought a minute. "I love to write."

"That's it!" Betty beamed. "Now, you get your pencil and paper and get started. Write your feelings down. Later, when your husband is better, you can read your story to him."

Obviously, Betty was trying. "I don't have paper with me. Besides I'll *never* forget this experience. If...when...Rick gets out of here, I'll just *tell* him about it."

"You know, dear," Betty persisted, "Trauma has an odd way of erasing its details from our memories. The mind protects itself from more than it can handle." She paused. "If you're a writer, jotting down your emotions and experiences will not only occupy your time but also give you something to be there for you later. Perhaps someday you'll use this ordeal to comfort others."

She patted Maggie's arm again and said, "Write your story."

Then Maggie was called to Rick's room for the allotted half-hour visit. She held his hand and whispered reassurances. All too soon, she had to trace her steps back to the waiting room.

Perched on the plum chair was a foil gift bag, tagged "Maggie." Curious, she opened it and pulled out a journal with an angel embossed on the cover.

I get the message, Betty, Maggie grinned. She reached in her purse for a pen and began to fill the blank pages.

⋈—◦—⋈

Angels are not freelance operators you can summon to cure your warts or make your horse win at the races. They come when God sends them, and when they come their purpose is to lead us closer to God. They're nonthreatening, wise and loving beings. They offer help whether we ask for it or not. But mostly we ignore them.

EILEEN ELIAS FREEMAN

⋈—◦—⋈

Father, I think about the moments in my life when you changed me. I think about the words that were spoken that gave me a new perspective, a new direction. I think about the angels who stepped into my life and were used by you to show me the way.

I think about all these things, and I am grateful. I think about all these words and moments, and I am filled with confidence that you have led me on my way.

THE MESSENGER PONY

Sophie was not a beach person, even though she had grown up only a Friday night's drive from the Atlantic shore. Many of her childhood weekends had been spent in the family car in standstill traffic on the Bay Bridge, the only route across the Chesapeake to Maryland's Eastern shore. Sophie had never liked broiling in oil under a hot sun or getting sand in her food, and she could not abide crowds. To her the beach usually meant getting a sunburn, and it held other dangers as well: sharks, jellyfish, crabs, and the pounding surf, with an undertow that sometimes threatened to yank her out to sea.

In spite of all this, the ocean was where she decided to go one day when she needed to make an important decision.

She borrowed a tent and, with her big dog Ruby, went to Assateague Island. She sat on the beach pondering change: marriage, children, and commitment. There was so much to think about, and Sophie didn't want to make a mistake. After dutifully making lists of pros and cons, Sophie pushed everything from her mind and ran into the surf. Ruby joined her, and when the two emerged from the waves, Sophie felt renewed, though she still had found no answers. She lay back on her towel, letting herself be lulled to sleep by the rhythms of sea and wind.

That evening, a wild pony galloped through her campsite, then paused on a grassy dune, standing outlined against the setting sun. The pony stamped its hoofs, snorted at her barking dog, turned its head into the breeze—and was gone. Sophie was in awe of what she'd just seen. She wondered if it was a sign. If so, what did it mean? That she, too, should continue to run free? Or, maybe the pony had stamped its feet and snorted to tell her, "Stop writing lists and follow your heart!" Then again, perhaps it was simply a wild pony, running free.

Sophie was not certain just when it was that she made her decision, but on her next camping trip with Ruby to Assateague Island, she brought her new husband, and she was expecting her first child.

God of all words and of the angels, I kneel before you in wonder at the ways you speak to me. Help me to hear your message in words, in deeds, in thoughts, in relationships, in nature. Let me, in all things and at all times, be open to your message for my life.

Angel voices, ever singing
Round Thy throne of light,
Angel harps, forever ringing,
Rest not day nor night.

FRANCIS POTT

Guiding Angels

Sweet souls around to watch us still,
Press nearer to our side;
Into our thoughts, into our prayers,
With gentle helpings glide.

HARRIET BEECHER STOWE

There are airy hosts, blessed spectators,
sympathetic lookers-on, that see and know
and appreciate our thoughts and feelings
and acts.

HENRY WARD BEECHER, ROYAL TRUTHS

TURNABOUT'S FAIR PLAY

School was starting in less than a month
when the Robinsons moved. Johnny's new
high school was a monstrous affair of attached
glass buildings full of sports trophies. Johnny, a
bookworm type of kid who wore glasses, was
not impressed. But, then, the few kids he'd met
weren't all that impressed with him either.

Teen years are hard enough with people you've
known all your life. With strangers, it's really
grim. Johnny had discovered, however, that
truancy and small mischief making earned him
a notoriety of sorts.

One Saturday morning, Johnny was hanging
around some of the tougher guys shooting
basketball in the park across the street from his
house. He'd had his hands on the basketball
only twice all morning. But, at least, he'd
consoled himself, he hadn't broken any laws
and nobody had beaten him up—yet.

And then Johnny looked up—his fate as a geek
was about to be sealed. Here came his elderly
neighbor, Frances. After walking rapidly down
the street—her gait like a bird chasing a seed—

she stopped in front of Johnny. "I would like you to come over tonight and meet some people," she said.

Johnny hesitated. "I already cleared it with your parents," she said with a surprisingly piercing gaze that held just a hint of laughter.

Johnny thought he was done for. He promised to mow the lawn, walk the dog, take out the garbage, and even tutor his youngest sister in math if his parents would not make him go over to Frances's house. They stood firm.

At any rate, when Johnny arrived, he encountered an unlikely group of friends that boasted this elderly lady as its center. Fragile as a violet in a flowing purple dress, Frances was surrounded by teenagers in assorted shapes, styles, and moods. There were geeks like him, but there were also kids who were considered "cool."

"I'd like you to meet Johnny," Frances said, pulling him toward her. "I think he has interesting plays to share with us. Perhaps we can each read a part to help him see how they'll work onstage."

Johnny looked at her, his mouth agog: His writing was a secret.

Frances, as he discovered, wasn't just any old lady, she was a best friend to teens who met once a week at her house to do homework, to play cards, or simply to talk. Nothing shocked her. Eventually the teens all simply gave up trying to be tough and enjoyed her friendship.

The first person ever to act in one of Johnny's musicals was Frances.

A messenger of love, she gently drew it from the teens, too, guiding them to become the people she knew they could be. Strangely, though, she always insisted they were angels sent to her, keeping her alert, vigorous, and she said, " ...young at heart."

Ten years later, Johnny read from his newest play for Frances. It was the least he could do. For today was her funeral at the church she loved. He took his place in front of an impromptu choir formed of many of the people who'd gathered at Frances's house all those years ago.

And they began to sing. The melody was simple so no rehearsal had been necessary—it was their final good-bye to Frances. As if inspired, their voices rose in sweetest song, sounding just a little bit like an angel chorus singing for one of their own.

I am going to send an angel in front of you, to guard you on the way and to bring you to the place that I have prepared. Be attentive to him and listen to his voice; do not rebel against him, for he will not pardon your transgression; for my name is in him.

*E*xodus 23:20–21

In this day and age, angels are more likely to appear in street clothes than in long white robes and halos. A neighbor who offers sound advice, a mentor who shows us how to live well, a friend who comforts us—can all be angels. If we live open to the possibility that God will use those

around us to guide our way, then we may
benefit from the guidance our earthly
angels give. We may not hear harps
playing or get goose bumps at the time,
but in hindsight we may give thanks for
God's angels on earth.

A SISTER TO GUIDE ME

When Anna remembers her childhood, she remembers her mother as acting sometimes full of joy and other times so despondent that she never left her room. Anna remembers ambulances taking her mother away for months and a doctor father who was also absent, although he was at work. Mainly, Anna remembers her big sister Theresa who, even though she was only four years older, had raised her.

Little Theresa was the one who made sure baby Anna got her bottle before bed, the one who changed her diapers, and the one who taught her to use the little potty. Theresa made them food, and when they ran out of milk, cereal, or peanut butter, she called their father and told

him what to buy at the store. Theresa taught
Anna to read, and when their father came
home after a late night, he often found them
asleep in each other's arms with a book in
between them.

When Anna went to her first high school dance,
it was Theresa who dragged their father from
his medical journals to take photos. And when
Anna came home after a party smelling of
cigarette smoke and alcohol, Theresa was the
one who sat her down to talk about the dangers
of peer pressure, alcohol, drugs, and boys.

By the time Anna was a senior in high school,
Theresa was in her last year of college. One
night, Theresa had just come home from the
library when the phone rang.

"Hey, I'm at this party...," Anna whispered,
sounding frightened as she related her situation.
Everyone was drinking, so she'd asked her date
to take her home. But the boy—a high school
football star—got angry and threatened that if
she squealed about the booze the team
members would be suspended, and she would
be sorry.

"I'll be right there," Theresa promised, wondering what she would do with a bunch of belligerent football players. When she got to the party, Theresa ignored the aggressive stares from some of the young men and marched straight to her sister. "Anna!" she said loudly, "You know you were grounded tonight. You get yourself on home before Dad finds you gone!" She grabbed her startled sister and pulled her from the room.

"Thanks!" Anna laughed as they drove away. "Now they won't be worried I'll say anything about the party!" Then she sighed, "I was so stupid—I thought those people were my friends!"

"Well, I hope you learned something," Theresa said, thankful it hadn't been worse.

"Yeah," Anna said, "Where would I be without you to guide me? Hey, I mean it," she smiled warmly.

God, I am a child no longer, yet I still know the need to have someone take me by the hand and lead me out of a scary place. Throughout my life you've sent those people to me, and together we have found the way. Bless those angels, Lord. May they find the hands to hold when they need them. Amen.

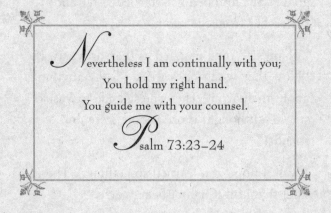

*N*evertheless I am continually with you;
You hold my right hand.
You guide me with your counsel.

*P*salm 73:23–24

ERRANDS WITH DAD

Although his father was decidedly a family man, there had been little opportunity for Gary to spend time with him as he was growing up. His father was a teacher who wanted to shower his family—his wife, four daughters, and one son—with extras, which forced him to moonlight constantly to supplement his income. Gary's dad was a blur of motion: taking tickets at football games, working as a security guard at the local newspaper, teaching night school, and grading endless papers.

Because Gary's mom didn't drive and the family could only afford one car anyway, it fell to Gary's dad to do most of the household errands on Saturday morning. That was Gary's time with his dad and he loved to go along.

His father took his errand running seriously. He insisted on taking an umbrella if it looked like rain and on Gary bringing "a good warm jacket" if it was cold outside. Before they left, his dad drove Gary's mom nearly to distraction about her grocery list. Whole pecans or pieces? What did she mean, "whatever fruit looked good"?

The errands always began with a fill-up at Tegeler's service station, the only place where his dad would buy gas even if it was a little more expensive. He explained that this was because the owner and mechanic, Bill, had always so tenderly doctored the family's ancient Chevrolet.

At their regular stops, his dad called everybody by name. If he knew them well enough, he'd ask about their kids or hobbies. He always thanked them for whatever service they rendered.

Once, his dad's courtesy got him into trouble. At a four-way stop, he was about to take his turn when he saw an acquaintance, Joe, at one of the other corners. His dad waved Joe on, and Joe sailed into the intersection—right into a fender bender. Later, Gary witnessed Joe giving his dad a hard time about it. His dad gently remonstrated, "Accepting a courtesy does not mean you shouldn't look both ways."

Sometimes on the way home, if there was enough time before his father went to his Saturday job, he took Gary to the parking lot of the high school and showed him how to drive. When Gary was very small, he "drove" sitting on his dad's lap. By the time he was old enough to get a permit, Gary was already a fine driver.

When Gary was 15, a Saturday came when he declined his dad's invitation to go on errands for the first time. Dad looked a little hurt until Gary explained that there was a big history test on Monday and that a girl with a beautiful smile had asked him over to study. Dad told him, "Be nice to her."

By that time, quite without realizing it, Gary had already absorbed the lessons those Saturday mornings had to offer: preparedness, attention to detail, loyalty, courtesy, responsibility, respect, and perhaps most of all, the simple pleasures of companionship.

***

All God's angels come to us disguised.
JAMES RUSSELL LOWELL

WIPED OUT

"I'm living my mother's life," Diane sighed. Two years into widowhood, her mother had been fighting for survival in the man-world previously cruised by Diane's dad. At the crossroads of midlife, Diane felt stuck in the same mire, fighting to lose her dependence—to take over the driver's seat and map out a new route.

While her mother learned to update license plates, tend flat tires, and maneuver through a car wash, Diane determinedly drove a parallel path. Each week she passed a mile marker in her own quest for independence.

One dreary day, Diane hesitantly braved that most macho domain, an auto parts store, to purchase rubber windshield wiper replacements for her car.

"What do you drive?" the sales assistant asked.

"A little car."

"What kind?"

"White," she answered.

"No. I need the make and model."

"It's a Honda Civic."

"Style?" Diane didn't know; those details belonged to her husband. So she dashed to the parking lot to read the label on the trunk. Back in the store she patted her hair into place while the man finished with another customer.

"DX," she puffed at the counter, brushing aside her drooping do.

Satisfied, he led her down an aisle and introduced her to a computer. Diane conquered the intricacies of entering vital auto data only to discover no "DX" listing. She traipsed the other aisles to relocate the sales assistant.

"What do I do now?"

"Bring in a wiper," he said, "and we'll be able to match it."

Shivering in the drizzle, she chipped two fingernails, broke a paper clip, and bent a key attempting to dislodge the blade. No luck.

Diane hunted down her clerk—again. This time, he sent her into the downpour with a sample wiper to compare sizes.

"It's about two inches longer than one blade and a half-inch longer than the other," she said, trying to fluff her matted hair. He pawed through the display.

"Sorry, ma'am, we don't carry that size."

"What size?" she nearly yelled, desperate for some information to take with her from this 30-minute episode. But he had walked away. Discouraged, Diane slouched, glared at the tidy rows of blades, and wrung out her hair.

A second clerk—a teenager—approached.

"May I help you?"

After listening to the roughly sketched details of Diane's dilemma, the employee smiled.

"If you're willing to buy the entire replacement blade, we have those in stock."

Would she! The blades were quickly located and, yes, courteously (perhaps even sympathetically) installed, all by a 16-year-old sales clerk who also happened to be a female.

Can Diane remove a blade now? Maybe. Does she know what size replacement she needs? No. Will she know how to install a windshield wiper next time? Probably not.

But, no longer is she as fearful of the journey. Diane knows that she is capable of changing gears, following detours, and mapping new routes in her life. She even manages to laugh at those moments when a little dignity is sometimes shed along with her dependence.

And, just think—all this thanks to the help and example of a resourceful teen angel.

Help me to be open to your guidance, Lord, however it comes. When you speak to me in the words of a friend, open my ears. When you touch me in the embrace of a family member, let me feel your gentle touch. And when you come to me in the almost imperceptible rush of angels' wings, alert my senses to your presence.

PLANE AND SIMPLE

Curtis fled to the garage—a retreat they often shared—and plunked onto the scarred swivel stool near the workbench. Granddad glanced up.

"Got a problem?" Sliding a weathered, knotty pine plank across two sawhorses, he balanced the unfinished board and steadied it with his knee.

Curtis shrugged and eyed the mist of sawdust and fragrant shavings that carpeted the workshop floor. He watched Granddad's thick fingers grip the ebony knob of a carpenter's plane as he leaned his weight into it. His long, even strokes and the rhythmic scrrrr-itch of metal blade against raw wood soothed his temper.

His grandfather paused. "Ready to talk?"

"Oh, Granddad, all I need is a new pair of sneakers. Is that too much to ask?"

"What did your mom say?"

"That the brand I want is too expensive. That the pair I have is good enough. That I need to learn money doesn't grow on trees. That...."

"I get the picture," he interrupted. His calloused palm brushed at the thin wooden curls, letting them drift to the concrete floor.

"Look here, son. This board is as smooth as silk now." He nodded toward the pile of lumber in the corner. "But until I worked it over, it looked just like those—warped, rough, even ugly. But now, well, it'll do."

Granddad's hand caressed the satiny length of the newly planed plank. "You know, Curtis, the happiest people don't necessarily have the most expensive things." Setting the wood aside, he slid another rough plank in its place.

"Seems to me, son, that the happiest people," scrrrr-itch, "are the ones who make the best of everything they have." With a broad wink, he handed him a plane. "Here, I think you need the practice."

Curtis ducked his head as a smile stole across his lips. *With a good washing and a new pair of laces*, he thought, *his old shoes might be okay after all.*

><+>-O-<+><

May we always recall and be thankful
For guiding lights along the way,
For the mentors and teachers who
  shaped us
Into the people we are today.

When we are sometimes feeling alone, assailed by outside forces, unsure of which way to go, it is comforting to think of angels watching over us, providing celestial support and guidance.

When at night I go to sleep,
Fourteen angels watch do keep:
Two my head are guarding,
Two my feet are guiding,
Two are on my right hand,
Two are on my left hand,
Two who warmly cover,
Two who o'er me hover,
Two to whom 'tis given
To guide my steps to heaven.

E. HUMPERDINCK

A MEMORABLE EQUATION

Jenny was a wonderful student in art and history, but by the end of her first year in high school, she had already had such disastrous experiences with math that she elected to take algebra in summer school. That way she could concentrate on it and possibly even do well—or at least pass. She knew it was natural for teachers to lose interest in students who struggle in the subject they teach. Yet it hurt her when she felt that her inability to understand had triggered in her former math teachers something close to disgust.

So it was with some nervousness that she went to her first class. She soon realized that Mr. Anderson treated her with the same interest and courtesy as the quicker students. He was an expert at reading faces, and when he saw Jenny's puzzlement, he approached the explanation from a different angle rather than repeating the same thing more loudly, as the other teachers had done. When Mr. Anderson saw tears spring to Jenny's eyes after he returned a paper in which she got two correct out of ten, he praised her for turning it in so promptly.

Though he surely had something better to do on those stifling July mornings when class was over, he never seemed rushed after the other students left when he sat beside her, trying yet another way to help her understand the subject.

The light never did turn green for Jenny in algebra, and Mr. Anderson was not able to give her that B he had urged her to strive for. She accepted his regretful C with great relief and gratitude. Later she would reflect that he probably wouldn't remember her at all and certainly not as one of his successes. She would never know a "binomial" from a "quadratic," but with Mr. Anderson's gentle help she had learned one very important equation:

Respect + Patience = Absolute Value.

Angels never tire of telling you that you are not alone.

Angels never tire of reminding you that you are loved and valued.

Angels never tire of affirming your life and your gifts.

SEASONS OF ANGELS

Through it all the angels dance,
Falling leaves and blooming flowers,
Summer's heat and winter's hours,
The ebb and flow of life.

Through it all the angels dance,
Inviting us to dance along,
Or at least to know the song,
Each season of our lives.

⊷⊷⊶○⊷⊶⊶

How lovely, God, is the newness of the
life around me. Flower buds peek out
from so many places. It's easy to imagine
an angel behind every one breathing life
and sending good energy to the world.
Give me eyes to see. Give me a heart to
respond.

The Love of His Gift

Angels appear to us in times of sorrow and grief to help us mend our broken hearts. After hearing his father's story, David was convinced of it.

David has many fond childhood memories and considers himself very lucky to have been raised by two special parents. His mom and dad were devoted to one another; she was the love of his dad's life. They raised their three sons with warmth and humor, and they gave them a home filled with love and security.

David's mother battled emphysema, and during the last two years of her life she was confined to a respirator. His dad was always there for her, and as she became ill their roles gradually reversed. He did the shopping, cooking, and cleaning, caring for David's mother as she had done for him all the years prior. He never complained and seemed happy for the chance to care for his beloved wife. One night, she died peacefully in her sleep.

David and his brothers tried to comfort their father as they all mourned together. A few days after their mother died, their dad said to them, "You know, I've never been alone. I went from home to college, into the Navy, then I married your mother. This is the first time I've been on my own." He was 73 years old. He missed her terribly.

David's folks lived in a city that had a music and crafts festival on the main street every summer. His parents had always enjoyed this event—strolling and enjoying the music, viewing the art displays, and delighting in the general air of friendliness and fun. Once again, the festival was in town, but David's dad wondered if he'd enjoy it alone. He decided he needed to get out and mingle with people to combat his grief and take his mind away from the solitary life he was now experiencing.

The day of the festival, David's dad walked up and down the crowded streets, enjoying the sights, sounds, and smells, but as the heat intensified he found himself getting a little weary. He began to look for a sidewalk café where he could sip lemonade and catch his breath.

He heard a voice call out to him, "Excuse me, sir, would you like to sit down?" He turned to find a pretty young woman smiling and motioning to a chair next to hers.

He graciously accepted her offer, and they began talking about the fair, the weather, and other general things that strangers chat about.

As he and the young lady conversed, she asked if he was married. He smiled sadly and began reminiscing about his wife. His sorrow and sense of loss were apparent, and the young lady listened attentively.

After chatting a while, she smiled and reached into the shopping bag she'd set at her feet. She presented David's dad with a gift, saying, "I bought this for myself because I collect angels, but I'd be delighted if you would accept this. I believe it was intended for you." In her hands was a small porcelain angel, sitting and mending a broken heart.

As David's dad recounted this story to David a few days later, they both realized that it had not been a chance meeting. An angel had entered the world of David's father with a gift to heal his broken heart.

David's dad passed on not long after the encounter. He had played a round of golf (his "second love") and followed it as usual with an afternoon nap. He passed away in his sleep, and his heart was finally mended as he rejoined his wife, the love of his life.

As for that angel with the broken heart . . . it is David's most valued possession.

Loving God, help us to sense your angelic messengers whenever and wherever and however they come to us. In the darkness of winter, the brightness of spring, the abundance of summer, the transitions of autumn, may we expect to be visited by your heavenly beings. And when those visits happen, may our eyes be open and our gratitude heartfelt.

ANGELS IN THE TREES

The sun had just risen on one of the first green days of the spring season. Anna, a young shutterbug trying to create a niche for herself in animal photography, couldn't wait to go to the secluded park her friend had told her about. Her friend had said the park had a forest as thick and deep and magical as the ones in a Brothers Grimm fairy tale. Anna was hoping that with the foliage so fresh and the park so far off the beaten path, only the tracks of animals would have marked the delicate blanket of forest floor.

Very early in the morning, she laced up her hiking boots, filled a thermos with coffee, and loaded her gear into her truck. When the asphalt of the county road gave way to gravel, Anna felt her anticipation mount. She could see the dark silhouettes of the trees up ahead. After parking in a clearing, she took a path into the woods. She was delighted by the moss that was beginning to collect at the bases of the evergreens; enchanted by the watchful doe that stood still until she heard the click of Anna's shutter and then fled.

Anna shot her first roll in no time and realized she hadn't brought extra film with her on the hike. She walked back to her truck to warm up and reload. Looking through the film, she noticed that she had brought only black-and-white film, including the roll she was removing from her camera. She was disappointed; she had hoped to catch the colors of the animals against the spring forest in her photography. A little upset, she decided to go back home and return another day.

A few months later after submitting many colorful photos to different animal magazines and ultimately getting rejected, Anna went to her darkroom to develop the black-and-white roll of film. In a photo with the light streaming through some trees, she thought she saw a pair of wings lightly etched in an evergreen's bark. She couldn't send it to an animal magazine, but on a whim she decided to submit it to a major photography magazine.

Months later, the picture graced the cover. She had called it "Angels in the Trees."

Green grass and blossoms blanket the
    earth,
For spring is the season of renewal and
    rebirth.
Tender buds, woodland creatures, new life
    without end—
How much of this do we owe to our many
    angel friends?

Yours is the day, yours also the night;
you established the luminaries and the sun.
you have fixed all the bounds of the earth;
you made summer and winter.

Psalm 74:16–17

Every blade of grass has an angel bending
over it saying, "Grow, grow."

THE TALMUD

ALL IS BRIGHT

Jill recalled in vivid detail the Christmas of 1978, or rather the week prior to that holiday, when she was a little girl.

Baking seasonal treats to deliver to neighbors was a tradition in Jill's family. It was also as much of an exercise in organization as it was a lesson in cooperation when Jill's mother marshaled all eight children into the kitchen one December evening.

"Bessie, I'm putting you in charge of both the cookie batter and the twins. Here is the recipe. Here are the twins.

"Ruth, I think you can manage to find and gather sprinkles, red hots, and chocolate chips to decorate with.

"Boys, come with me, and I'll teach you the art of making your Granny's special frosting."

As the six-year-old caboose of the family, Jill was dubbed Jill-of-all-trades and ended up being the official helper. Oh, how she loved helping!

Jill helped Bessie and the twins:

"I know Daddy likes crispy cookies, but get those eggshells out of my batter!" demanded Bessie.

Jill helped Ruth:

"Absolutely no rubber-band haloes on these cookies," Ruth insisted.

Jill helped her mother and the boys:

"No, I don't think eight cups of sugar is better than two," said her mother.

The mixing, cutting, baking, and icing took them well into the night. Finally, all the mixing bowls, spoons, and baking sheets had been washed and put away. All the flat surfaces had been wiped clean of spills. All the cookies had been cut and decorated and set aside. Jill's mother dug out her giant plastic bowls.

Gingerly, each sweet treat was lifted. Proudly, each work of art was admired. Not a star was chipped, not a halo cracked. After they filled and stacked three huge containers, Jill grabbed the last lid and stretched all the way across the counter to help . . . and bumped her elbow.

Down came the pile—bowls, cookies, and all.

Talk about "Silent Night." They all stared at the floor. Then everybody looked at Jill. No one said a word for a solid minute. Which was exactly enough time for Jill to race to her bedroom and bury her head under a pillow.

Then, through her sobs, Jill heard her mother crooning as she rubbed Jill's back. At last Jill quieted enough to listen. Only she didn't hear the lecture that she deserved and expected from her tired, disappointed parent.

"Don't cry," her mother said. "They're just cookies."

Gathering Jill in her arms, her mother tucked her head under her chin and began to hum as she rocked Jill. Then she started to chuckle.

That couldn't be. Suspicious, Jill pulled herself back and looked up—right into her mother's smiling face.

"Are you *laughing?*"

"Yes," said her mother. "I certainly am. After all, in 25 years we'll laugh about this, so why wait? Why don't you and I go ahead and laugh now?"

"Now?"

"Now."

Jill smiled through her tears. And she vividly remembers how they made a shimmering halo around her mother's head.

A lot of Christmases have come and gone since then. So many, in fact, that this Christmas Jill will follow family tradition and make holiday cookies with her own little helper. But the memory of that particular Christmas doesn't dim with time. It only gets brighter.

Angels can fly because they can take themselves lightly.

G.K. CHESTERTON, ORTHODOXY

There is no one time or place
When angels can appear.
They come when needed,
Filled with grace
To those who God holds dear.

Father, the wind rustling the leaves
reminds me of angel wings all around me.
Thank you for such a reminder. Help me
to stay mindful that the work of angels
goes on all the time all around me whether
I am aware or not, and that life is even
more than I see.

JUST PASSING BY

Kathy settled herself on the couch with a cup of lemon spice tea and stacks of papers about cars. She needed a new car. Her heart, however, wasn't in the search.

It wasn't just a matter of money, although finances were always a major consideration. It was a matter of sentiment.

Each time Kathy passed the old station wagon, she would pat its crumpled side with the affection usually reserved for good friends. It was in the confines of this car that she had met someone even more special.

Six months earlier, during a winter blizzard, Kathy's car had spun off an icy road in a series of graceful pirouettes and come to rest in a deep, snow-filled ditch.

Fortunately, there were no other cars around to get tangled up with, but that also meant no one would likely be coming along for hours. This was Kathy's usual shortcut on country back roads between her house and the courthouse in town where she was a circuit court judge.

Used to weighing the facts and options of each situation, Kathy knew this one was not good: First, the pressure on her chest from the steering wheel where she was jammed would kill her if the subzero temperature didn't do it first. Second, the airbag had deflated as quickly as it expanded and was threatening to suffocate her. And third, no matter how much she wriggled, she couldn't move enough to reach her cell phone to call for help.

She had no idea how long it had been since the accident, but she knew that the deepening lethargy creeping through her body was a warning that she was about to lose consciousness. She drifted in and out of awareness, so cold that she could no longer shiver.

Suddenly, a man—ordinary looking in denim coveralls, a hooded parka, and a red-checked hat—appeared beside her car.

"Are you okay, lady?" he asked.

She could only nod, not having enough room to inhale deeply for a shout.

"We'll have you out of there in a minute," he said.

Before she could whisper, "Thank you," he disappeared.

She didn't see him return but heard a noise behind her. Glancing up in the rearview mirror, she saw him shoveling snow away from the exhaust. Of course—the carbon monoxide would have killed her even before the cold or the steering wheel's pressure.

"Sit still now," the man said, shouting through the back window. "I'm going to be making some noise."

And, with that, she heard a wrenching sound as the rear station wagon door reluctantly opened. The man crawled in and appeared behind her.

Carefully, he lowered the car's seat back and helped her slide out to safety. He held her in his arms and let her take in several deep breaths.

"We've got to keep moving," he said.

Half pushing, half carrying her, the man got her up the steep embankment to the roadside. An ambulance was just pulling up behind a farm livestock truck; she could smell the reassuringly familiar aroma of cows. Gently the man set her down on the ground. She closed her eyes lightly as she waited for the EMTs. She opened her eyes again when she felt a blanket being wrapped around her.

"I'm so glad he called you," Kathy said to the EMT who was gently stabilizing and strapping her onto the stretcher.

"Who?" said the EMT, looking around in confusion. "Nobody called. We were dispatched to another accident, but then we got the signal to disregard it. We just happened to be passing by."

When Kathy's husband went to the accident scene later that afternoon, the snowfall had erased any trace of an angel who'd worn a red-checked hat and driven a stock truck.

Father God, the earth is asleep. The buds of spring lie in wait. The wonder of your world seems in a holding pattern just waiting for the go-ahead to grow. Let winter teach us the value of stillness, of silence, and of meditation. Help us to know that angel wings don't have to flutter wildly to do the work of your kingdom of peace.

⊰─◆─◇─◆─⊱

Silently, one by one, in the infinite meadows of heaven
Blossomed the lovely stars, the forget-me-nots of angels.
  HENRY WADSWORTH LONGFELLOW, EVANGELINE

GARDEN ANGEL

"There," Cassie said as she placed the alabaster angel in the center of the blooming wildflowers, "my garden is now perfect!"

"Well," said her friend Ali, "it is truly beautiful, well designed, and peaceful. But won't it be just a wee bit uncomfortable next winter?"

Cassie smiled. "It's a garden for all seasons; when the weather's bad, I'll just look at my angel from inside the house," she pointed through the nearby picture window. "I could even have a fire in the hearth!"

That was 20 years ago, and Cassie's words had been prophetic. Her garden angel had been a comforting presence through the hard times, an affirming one in the good. While sitting on her cushioned bench in the garden, Cassie had welcomed the dawn on humid summer mornings, inhaled the crisp scent of autumn, enjoyed the peaceful hush of winter snow, and rejoiced in the renewal of spring. And, when harsh winds chilled and rain and sleet fell, she'd contemplate from behind her window how the cycle of life played out year after year around the angel in her garden.

While she'd rocked her newborn twins in the garden that first spring, the dogwood trees near the little angel had also brought forth new buds. In summers, when the angel sat in the riot of wildflowers, Ellen had sought peace in her garden while the rest of the yard was a clamor of wild children, unleashed from school. On her 50th birthday last fall, auburn chrysanthemums bloomed behind the angel, in mocking contrast to the waning pigment in her own graying hair. And when a mantle of snow draped the outside angel in a blanket of white, Ellen sat behind her window wrapped in an afghan her grandmother had made years ago.

How true, she often reflected, were these words:

> "For everything there is a season, and a time for every matter under heaven: a time to be born, and a time to die; a time to plant, and a time to pluck up what is planted" (Ecclesiastes 3:1–2).

I need you, God, in all the seasons of my life. I need your angels gathered around me. I need to believe you care for me in all my ages and stages. Give me the faith that reminds me I don't have to go it alone. Bless me with whispers of angels in my life, until the end of my days.

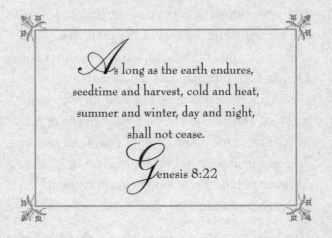

As long as the earth endures,
seedtime and harvest, cold and heat,
summer and winter, day and night,
shall not cease.

Genesis 8:22

~ Chapter Seven ~

ANIMALS AS ANGELS

*The animals in our lives—who of us can
understand the ways they use to care for us?
They are companions, affectionate friends,
nonjudgmental housemates. And who can say if
they might not also be ministering angels?*

>─◄◆►─○─◄◆►─<

*I love those angel animal friends
Who are by my side every day,
My love grows stronger evermore
For those with whom I share the way.*

CAT SPEAK

Ralph volunteered to string the Christmas lights on the outer row of trees of his subdivision. He brushed aside his neighbors' thanks. As a building contractor, it was no big deal for him to climb up a ladder, even during the cold December weather. In fact, he rather enjoyed the time to himself, reflecting on the joys of the season and the blessings that filled his life. His cat, Sky, had followed him out there.

He was standing on one of the highest rungs, reaching to hook a strand around a branch at the back of a tall tree, when he lost his balance. He fell to the frozen ground with a sickening crunch, landing with his leg folded behind him. Searing pain gripped him when he tried to move.

"My leg's broken," Ralph moaned. The only question was whether he could make his way home. Gingerly trying to pull his leg out from under him, he grimaced in pain. There was no way he could even move, let alone make it all the way back to the road where someone could see him.

"Someone will come along," he told himself, trying to think positively despite the gathering dusk and deepening cold. He rubbed his hands together, attempting in vain to keep his hands warm. Sky nuzzled his face and meowed uneasily.

"Very tired...I'll just rest," Ralph mumbled to himself. Almost as soon as he dozed off, a persistent sound brought him back. "That darn cat, always meowing..."

"Go home, Sky," murmured Ralph. He hoped his weak command would send his cat on her way, and maybe his family would realize something was wrong when they saw her. "Go home."

Looking cowed, Sky skittered off. *Probably headed straight to her favorite spot by the fireplace,* Ralph thought, shivering uncontrollably.

But Sky ran straight to Ralph's backyard and started meowing. She wouldn't stop, even when Ralph's family let her in and petted her. She kept up the shrill, incessant meowing, looking at them reproachfully and pawing at the back door.

Cynthia, Ralph's wife, came to the back door to see what the commotion was about. Sky meowed even louder and pawed the door.

"You crazy cat!" Cynthia exclaimed, exasperated. "Is there something out there you want? What is it—a bird?"

Cynthia opened the door and Sky ran outside. She crossed half the backyard before running back, stopping in front of Cynthia and meowing.

"What is it?" Cynthia said. Looking at the clock, she said, "It's not quite time for your dinner..." Then she realized that Ralph should have been home almost an hour ago. "Oh, no," she said. "Where's Ralph? Sky, is that what you're trying to tell me?"

Cynthia quickly put on her coat and shoes and let Sky lead her across the backyard and over to Ralph. He was in pretty bad shape from the cold and pain. At the hospital, doctors set his leg and watched closely to be sure he regained full use of his frostbitten fingers.

That spring, Ralph sat on the patio and stretched his recently mended leg. Sky was lying on his lap. As usual, she was meowing at birds and squirrels and nothing in particular. "You meow all you want to, girl," Ralph said, petting his angel cat.

Always listen for an angel's voice; you'll speak more softly yourself.

A sleeping cat in the room is like candlelight—the world feels safer and life seems more delightful.

PUPPY LOVE

The kids begged for a puppy. They would take care of it. They would feed it. They would housebreak it, teach it tricks, take it for walks. Finally, their mom and dad gave their consent, and the family adopted Blitzen, a midnight-black toy poodle.

Who wouldn't love a palm-sized, powder-puff puppy? Who wouldn't giggle over a furiously wagging stub of a tail? And who could resist cuddling that silky bundle? Blitzen made certain his "kisses" were equally distributed, his love shared with everyone.

No one could have foreseen the medical issues ahead. No one could have known this four-footed angel had a mission to carry out.

First it was hip dysplasia. Surgery followed, leaving Blitzen with one leg shorter than the others. He listed to the left. His lope was lopsided. Still, he ran joyfully to fetch sticks and stuffed toys. Like a high-jump champion, he learned to back up for both speed and loft in order to hurl himself onto one child's bed or another. He raced across the soccer field, somersaulting comically when his three good legs overcompensated for the fourth.

Then the seizures began. Mild shaking turned to full convulsions requiring consistent medication, watchful eyes, and floor cleanup. Yet the kids kept their word and took care of the dog.

They learned to hide his medication in cheese and took turns getting him outside at night, even standing barefoot in the snow, teary-eyed while he had the seizures. They cleaned up his messes. They kept his food and water dishes full. They tempted his dwindling appetite with tasty morsels from their own plates.

The children learned responsibility and more. They learned about determination, compassion, and tenderheartedness. They learned how to show unconditional love. Tending Blitzen throughout the years of his infirmities taught them an obligation to care for the weak. And when, at the end, they laid their ebony-furred friend to rest under a shady evergreen, they learned a final lesson from their well-loved pet: to revere life with all its frailties.

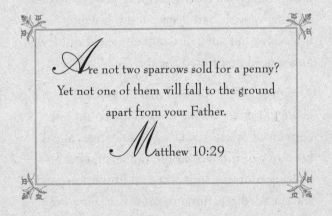

Are not two sparrows sold for a penny? Yet not one of them will fall to the ground apart from your Father.

Matthew 10:29

Thank you, God, for all the animals who have helped us feel closer to you and your creation. Keep them safe, these trusted innocents who calm our lives and show us love. Help them find their way home if they are lost. Help them hear the voices of those who will care for them. Save them from every unsafe place.

A DIFFERENT PATH

Ellen had been job hunting for two years, and though she was well educated and had many skills, she'd only recently been called for an interview. It had been a long, grueling interview, but she felt confident she'd done well and would be offered the job.

A high-pressure job like this one would be a big change, but try as she might, she could not convince herself it was a good change. She'd been out of the workforce for several years—waiting until the kids were all in school—and she dreaded returning to an office. However, she and her husband were already behind in saving for the children's future education, so she would take the job if it was presented.

Two weeks later Ellen was alone when the call came. Hearing it was the ad agency, she almost blurted, "I'll take it!" But instead of an offer, she was thanked for her interest and told the job had been accepted by someone else.

Devastated, Ellen leaned against the wall, then crumpled into a heap on the floor. What a failure she was, and an overconfident one at that. Tears of isolation and despair rolled down her cheeks.

Immediately, her dogs were all around, licking her tears and nuzzling her neck and arms. Crying harder, Ellen stroked their fur and hugged them; then, she started to laugh despite the tears.

"You dogs," she sniffled, "you're happy I'm unemployed because you love going for walks!" Too late, she realized her choice of words as the dogs ran to the door, took their leashes in their mouths, and watched her expectantly. She dried her tears and got up. She did love to take the dogs on long walks, playing and teaching them new tricks.

She drove to the park, needing a walk by the river. Soon the fresh air, moving water, and her furry friends put the job loss in perspective. Ellen laughed at the dogs' antics as they fetched, laid down, rolled over, stayed, and came on command. As they were playing, a woman approached.

"I see you have a way with dogs," she said approvingly. "I've been looking for a partner to open a dog walking and training business. Would you be interested?"

Ellen caught her breath. A chance to do work that was not only useful but fun? "I sure would!" she said, beaming.

Father, thank you for feathers and fur that cover the hearts of unexpected angels. Thanks for the softness between my fingers that reminds me of how my heart can grow. Thank you for the wonder they inspire, the smiles and laughter. Thank you for their touch and their ability to share. Everything that lives is holy, life delights in life.

WILLIAM BLAKE, "AMERICA: A PROPHESY"

APPALOOSA EARL

When Marcy first met Earl, she could tell he was a sweet guy. He was good-looking too, in a big, rangy appaloosa sort of way. He had a habit of flapping his lower lip when he was nervous, which made him seem quirky and especially cute to Marcy and her daughters. They themselves were sometimes a bit nervous, especially around big horses, and Earl was big.

Marcy had always wanted a horse. Not long after her 45th birthday, it occurred to her that if she was ever going to fulfill this dream, she couldn't wait much longer. Her girls were delighted.

Most of the horses they'd looked at seemed intimidating. Marcy had nearly decided that she was destined to back down and let this dream go unfulfilled when along came Earl. This horse didn't seem intimidating, at least not in the surroundings of the livery where they'd gone on a few trail rides to satisfy their horse hunger. And even in those circumstances, his kind, willing nature showed.

When they brought the horse home, reality set in: They had absolutely no idea how to handle a horse. Sure, it was no big deal to climb into the saddle at the livery, where the horses were led out already saddled. But it was another thing entirely to go into a field, catch a horse, and have to lift up each hoof to clean it out.

Earl picked up on their nervousness right away. Marcy and the girls didn't know it then, but the reason a nervous person makes a horse upset and flighty is because horse logic says: "If my human is scared, there must be something really awful out there that will try to get me." When self-preservation kicks in, even kind horses forget their manners, and 1,000 pounds of unmannerly animal is never good. It could have become a dangerous situation had it not been for their new friend, Samantha, who was nicknamed Sam.

Was it a heaven-sent coincidence that Sam had come into their lives on practically the same day they met Earl? Sam had grown up riding horses, she had once been a trainer, and she understood their ways. An astute observer of people, Sam also realized that though her new friend Marcy was desperate to have a horse, Marcy was totally unprepared. As Sam didn't want to see anyone get hurt, she stepped right in to help.

Sam overflowed with enthusiasm, optimism, and energy. She walked for hours beside Earl, giving both him and his riders confidence as he carried them around the field. She hiked great distances alongside the horse, always professing that she loved to walk. If a rider got scared or if Earl seemed insecure, Sam would climb aboard and help Earl and his new owners sort things out. She would remind Marcy what a kind, willing horse they had. Walking along, Sam would frequently remind the riders to "pet him on the withers—it really calms him down." And it worked.

Soon Marcy blossomed into a confident horsewoman, and the girls enjoyed competing in local shows. They bought several horses, but Earl remained everyone's favorite.

Some angels help in dramatic ways, while others help in ways that are more subtle but just as important. Marcy always feels a deep gratitude to Earl, not only because he helped her pull her dreams out of the trash but also because he brought into her life another true friend, Sam. Marcy's daughters will always be grateful that Earl was there for them during their turbulent teenage years so they could ride the appaloosa alone on days when the only company they could stand was his. Now almost 30, with poor eyesight, Earl continues to take care of people and help them fulfill their dreams.

The special animals we share our lives with
Know all about us—
And love us anyway.

God of all things, we thank you for all your creatures, from the largest to the smallest. In each of these wondrous animals, we see your creative touch. Help us to respect all you have created, to protect their lives, and to be ready to learn from them anything you would like to teach us.

DOING THERAPY

Sean had been trapped into spending part of his Saturday at a nursing home. He'd only agreed to go with the pet therapy people because the pretty girl in his government class said she'd be going. And now she wasn't even here.

Arriving at Hills Retirement Center, volunteers piled out of the vans with dogs on leashes and cats in carriers. Inside, someone handed Sean a scrawny kitten. It was a little yellow tabby with a loud voice.

The big community room was full of older people who started buzzing excitedly when they saw the animals. As the cats and dogs were brought closer, people started exclaiming, "Come here, boy!" "Oh, Isis, don't you look pretty!" "Hey, pup, where did you get that new collar?"

Sean hung back, not sure anyone would want to pet the scrawny kitten. Then he noticed one woman who sat alone, staring at her lap. As everyone else was busy, Sean went over and held out the kitten.

"His name's Tiger," Sean mumbled, making up the name on the spot. Then, not sure what else to do, he placed the kitten on her lap. The woman continued to sit still as a stone and didn't acknowledge him or the cat. Tiger started mewing and crawled around the woman's lap, clambering over her unmoving arms and licking her wrinkled hands.

"Hey, kid, don't bother with her," one of the center's aides told Sean. "Poor Greta doesn't talk or move, and I'm not even sure if she sees or hears."

Sean glared at the aide, thinking how awful it would be to have to listen to someone talking about you like that. Then, out of the corner of his eye, he noticed the kitten was about to fall off Greta's lap.

Before he could react, Greta's bony hand shot out and grabbed the kitten by the scruff of his neck and slowly, as if rediscovering arms she'd forgotten she had, secured the kitten up against her thin chest. Tiger yawned, then reached up a tiny paw and tentatively touched Greta's chin. And then...

"Look!" exclaimed a woman sitting nearby, "Our Greta smiled!"

Try as he might, Sean couldn't stop grinning on the van as they returned to town.

"See you next month, Sean?" asked the driver.

"You bet!" He grinned at the kitten curled in the crook of his arm, and Tiger began purring.

Lord, thank you for these angels who come to me in fluff and fur. Thank you for their magic of putting laughter in the hearts of those they love. Thanks for their trust and their unabashed desire to give affection and to be scratched behind the ears.

JUBILANT

An angel came to us once in the form of a
black Labrador puppy. My husband and I
had gone through a difficult time, and we
needed some joy. In came Jubilant, a furry
little bouncing ball of fresh perspective and
endless delight. She reminded us that life
is bigger than our problems; she kissed
away our defenses and played away our
uneasiness. She grew to be 60 pounds and
our hearts grew along with her. You may
call her a pet—we'll understand what you
mean. Sometimes, though, if I catch a
glimpse of Jubi out of the corner of my eye,
I think she's tucking in her wings so we
won't know. She's trying to keep us from
realizing she was sent to us to save us. She
has done well.

Free to a Good Farm Home

Dave was beginning to realize it had been foolish to think that he could keep an energetic Border collie as a pet in the city. Growing up on a sheep farm, he and his father had trained a succession of the black-and-white canines as herders, and they had been his best friends.

Now his dog Cookie was a year old. Despite the dog's splendid disposition, Dave's steadfast attempts to train her, and the daily hour-long walks the two enjoyed, she simply had too much energy to spend the day in a city apartment. Cookie chewed things. She jumped on visitors. She was so rambunctious that Dave could hardly drink a mug of the coffee he liked without Cookie's vigorously wagging tail overturning the cup.

Reluctantly, Dave made the decision that Cookie would be better off out in the country where she could frolic and run. Just as he was about to pick up the phone to call and place a classified ad, the phone rang, startling both of them. It brought the news that Dave's father, to whom

Dave had been very close, had died suddenly of a heart attack while doing farm chores.

The plans to find a new home for Cookie were put on hold as Dave attended to the sad details. At first his shock and grief were so overwhelming that, as he sat staring into space with a book on his lap, he barely noticed how much Cookie had calmed down.

Then he realized it had been weeks since she had misbehaved. Instead she sat quietly beside him as he remembered how his dad took him trout fishing and taught him how to take care of his gear. As Dave remembered his father, Cookie looked into his eyes with what he could have sworn was intelligent empathy. And even when she appeared to be dozing at his feet, a mere look from Dave was enough to make his dog raise her head to give him a soft lick on the hand or to gently wag her tail.

After the first stage of Dave's grief passed, Cookie regained some of her puppy energy, but she was never again out of control. And Dave felt a growing certainty that it was not merely coincidence that had kept him from placing that ad.

It's funny how dogs and cats know the inside of folks better than other folks do, isn't it?

ELEANOR H. PORTER, POLLYANNA

And God said, "Let the earth bring forth living creatures of every kind: cattle and creeping things and wild animals of the earth of every kind." And it was so. God made the wild animals of the earth of every kind, and the cattle of every kind, and everything that creeps upon the ground of every kind. And God saw that it was good.

Genesis 1:24–25

PEACE ANGELS

*May you awake each morning in the
presence of angels.
May you live each day with God's peace
in your heart.
When you fall asleep at night, may you know
peace within and without, that your dreams may
be filled with the sweet whispers of angels.*

◄►◄►○◄►◄►

*Peaceful angels rest among us,
Whispering secrets we can hear,
If we'll calm ourselves and listen,
Truth and grace will gather near.*

TAKING WING

A ngels. Multitudes of angels. Tens of thousands of angels. And they descended from everywhere. They flew from nearly every state; they winged their way from foreign countries. They soared from other continents. They arrived from nursing homes, synagogues, and hospitals. They came from schools, churches, universities, and civic organizations. This host of angels, one in purpose, converged and landed only a couple of months after the terrorist attacks of September 11, 2001. They had a message to deliver.

Like the people who created them and sent them, these angels were of every color and every creed and were full of character. Long, lean clothespin angels. Delicate seashell angels. Prickly pinecone angels. Angels made from craft sticks, steel wool pads, and macaroni. From tongue depressors, common muslin, and filmy tulle.

All were heart-conceived and handcrafted.

The idea itself was simple: Mail small holiday ornaments for the families of 9/11 victims. One little contagious plan that rapidly winged its way around the world, unifying people everywhere. And the only rule? Use inexpensive, common items lying around the house.

Spirited crafters took the challenge. Each angel was personalized, some in their unique style, a few with individual names, and others with handwritten messages. All the angels were sent with empathy, sympathy, and love for the families who would receive them in time for the holiday season—the first lonely Christmas after the tragic loss of their loved ones.

The angels arrived at their destinations in New York City, in Washington, D.C., and in Pittsburgh, Pennsylvania. Each was carefully lifted from its packing and lovingly delivered; and each was gratefully received by grieving families.

During that time of abject terror and deep mourning, a worldwide alliance of earthly angels banded to form a community and give wing to heavenly messengers—homespun angels of peace, comfort, and love.

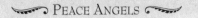
We can spread the angels' light of peace
by lighting one candle at a time all around
the world.

━━━◦━━━

Warfare rages round the world
In hamlet and in city,
As nations fail to recognize
Their need for unity.

We see our differences, the ways
We vary from each other,
Yet fail to see
Our common ties as sisters and as
  brothers.

Send down your angels, God above,
That we might know release.
Through their angelic love lead us
Toward your new realm of peace.

LEAN ON ME

It was the hardest column Elizabeth ever had to write. For a dozen years, she had been writing a weekly, humorous newspaper column based on the home life of her big and, she thought, happy family. Then came a sudden and painful divorce. She considered her options: quitting the column, writing it but not telling about the sea of change in her life, or letting the readers who had been loyal for a dozen years know when the bad times rock as well as when the good times roll.

She decided to trust the readers, writing, "I never thought I would be divorced. I don't even believe in divorce. But here I am, and in the end I concluded that, for better or worse, life has always been my beat. Although my family's privacy is paramount, so is being straight with you. I won't be writing about the 25th-anniversary trip we were planning, but instead about the joys and pains of raising teenagers alone.

"I'll likely address the challenges of handling with grace such events as our adult children's weddings and our future grandchildren's baptisms. I am already able to share the unexpected perk of The Amazing Divorce Diet: Lose Five Pounds in a Week Without Ever Leaving the Couch!

"Perhaps down the road I may be writing about the horrors of dating again as a spring lamb of 49. I hope you'll be patient with me, because I know that people in the throes of divorce are somewhere between not right and insufferable for at least a year."

Elizabeth had second thoughts during the wee hours of the day when the column would appear. Would people think she was a hypocrite or a fool for having written so glowingly about her family life when she should have been able to see that it was about to crumble? Would they think she had no business sharing such personal information? The little red numbers on her alarm clock changed at a glacial pace.

By 8:00 A.M., the phone was ringing with offers of comfort and support. At 10:00, the florist came up the walk with a big bouquet. For several weeks, she was overwhelmed by an outpouring of calls and cards. Readers sent e-mails complete with electronic hugs and songs, yoga techniques, centering prayers, Bible verses, divorce stories to share, books to read, sympathy chocolate cravings, and just plain kindness. One reader recommended healing through laughter and sent a rubber duck to help as she soaked the sorrow away. Someone sent a CD with the song "Lean on Me." The simplest messages went the most directly to her heart. One read: "Been there. Done that. Made it. So will you."

Perhaps most touching of all was the tallith, or Jewish prayer shawl, knitted by a reader who had said a prayer with every stitch. Elizabeth was to put it on many times in the difficult year to come. Every time, she felt herself surrounded by a mantle of peace.

Merciful God, my heart is heavy.
Visit me with angels, that I may receive
the peace that comes only from you.
And then, with the lightness of angelic
wings, may I lift my face to heaven to
receive your gift of new life.

THE DREAMS OF ANGELS

Dream of a world where people disagree
    but hold onto each other.
Dream of a world where respect and
    dignity are priorities for everyone.
Dream of a world where power and
    influence are valued as opportunities to
    do good.
Dream of a world where all children are
    free to laugh and play and imagine how
    to make the world a better place.

MEMORIES OF MARY

Will there be any potluck dinners in heaven? Mary's friends at St. Luke's Church hope so. Her heart was as big as she was. If you were hungry, unhappy, lonely, or upset, you went to the church's kitchen and warmed yourself at Mary's fire. Soon you found yourself with a brighter outlook and an inner peace.

At the church, Mary was as permanent a fixture as the giant coffeepot she kept perking at all times of the day. She created her own version of loaves and fishes every Wednesday night, making dinner for those who came for choir practice, meetings, and volunteer maintenance chores. She never knew how many were coming, but somehow there was always enough food. She made room at the table for everyone.

Mary had a gift. She was one of those rare cooks who could peer into a refrigerator, see three slices of stale bread, a couple of limp stalks of celery, some leftover stew, and a lone egg, and somehow visualize dinner.

Could Mary whip up a Cajun dinner for a Mardi Gras celebration? Might she arrange a "Franks Be To God" hot dog luncheon for the whole church on pledge Sunday? How about a bake sale for the youth group? Maybe some chili and ham sandwiches for the choir visiting from Africa? "Love to" was her typical reply.

Although she loved those group events, Mary enjoyed her one-on-one time with the church members and staff even more. If the church secretary or custodian had a particularly hectic day, Mary would insist that they take time to sit down for a lovely little meal of soup and toast and cookies, and then send them on their way, deeply refreshed.

Lent was a hard time for Mary because so many people gave up sweets. Indulging the sweet tooth of others was one of her greatest pleasures in life. During that time, the table in the fellowship hall looked bare without her tempting array of cakes and pies and cookies. As the weeks of Lent wore on, a generous dollop of whipped cream began to appear on the Jell-O, and Mary gradually began adding "salads," the chief ingredient of which was pistachio pudding.

Mary had a special connection to children. Besides her cookies and cherry pie, it was the way she talked to them, with genuine interest in their activities and a hearty laugh.

When those she left behind join her in heaven, God's going to have some explaining to do. How could he take her and leave them? Until they see her again, Mary's friends find it a comfort to imagine her no longer laboring to walk on painful, swollen feet but tripping lightly up the hill to the pearly gates. She has a wide smile on her face, and in her outstretched hand is a big sheet pan of Texas brownies for St. Peter. Inside, the angels are rolling up their sleeves and tying on their bibs, because the word is out on the celestial grapevine: Mary's coming home.

Angels are yet one more sign of God's goodness, a sign that God cares for us and uses many ways to express that love. Many people find peace in knowing that angels are watching over them.

Wrap yourself in the wings of an angel and you will find peace.

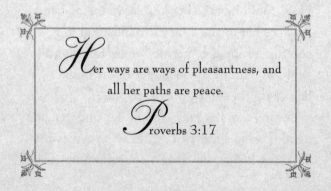

*H*er ways are ways of pleasantness, and
all her paths are peace.

*P*roverbs 3:17

SECRET MISSIONS

No one was certain who left it there. In fact, discussing the mystery was one of the more positive conversations the Taylor household had heard in a long time.

With seven yours-mine-and-ours kids in the house, dissension was at a record high. Teenage independence, pre-pubescent hormones, and preschool petulance made home life tumultuous at its worst and interesting at its best. Not one of the children was bad, but their blended household was still full of lumps.

And then the angel showed up.

There it sat, plump and sassy, perched among the cushions on the porch swing. Four-year-old Abbey was the one who found it. Made from fluffy white flannel, its cherubic face manifested a permanent smile, fetching an identical one from all the others as Abbey excitedly waved it through the house.

Pinned to the angel's flowing robe was a note:

> *I'm just a heavenly visitor*
> *Sent from up above*

To change the strife in your house
To unconditional love.

For someone else do something nice
Then leave me on their bed.
They, in turn, will pass me on
And peace will reign instead.

"I don't get it," growled 11-year-old Max.

"Oh, brother! You're the Boy Scout. You should be an expert on good deeds," taunted 15-year-old Kate. "That's what it means. Good deeds for each other. Probably in secret."

"Secret!" squealed Abbey. "I love secrets. Can I be first?"

While the older kids rolled their eyes, Mother nodded. "Yes, you can, Abbey. Just remember to leave the angel on the person's pillow so they'll know it's their turn next." She looked into each child's face and said in her no-nonsense voice, "And we'll all take a turn."

That's when the fun began. With a little direction from Dad, Abbey started the ball rolling. After lots of giggles and only trying out the lipstick once, she straightened Kate's makeup drawer. Then she left the smiling angel on her big sister's bed and didn't tell a soul.

Kate cleaned the master bathroom. Mother let Max sleep in and delivered his newspaper route in his place. Max washed Dad's car. Bicycles were repaired, beds mysteriously made, brownies baked, toys picked up—as the stuffed angel moved from pillow to pillow.

And that's when the magic began. Mother and Dad noticed it first: evidence of less bickering, more generosity, and newly expressed love. At long last, peace was seeping into the Taylor household, one good deed at a time.

And the angel kept smiling.

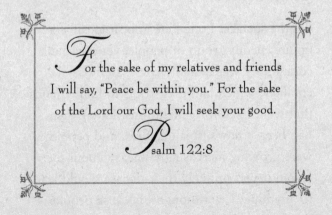

For the sake of my relatives and friends I will say, "Peace be within you." For the sake of the Lord our God, I will seek your good.

Psalm 122:8

Peace without and peace within,
Peace alone and with another,
Peace of heart, of soul, wherein
One knows one's blessings altogether.

MARTIN VISITS LONE PINE

Celia found it both heartening and interesting that her son's school would put on a play to commemorate Dr. Martin Luther King, Jr. In fact, when her family had moved to the rural Midwestern town of Lone Pine from a suburb of Washington, D.C., Celia had feared that her children would grow up with no appreciation for the diversity she'd taken for granted back East.

On the surface, Lone Pine appeared to be a homogeneous group of people, yet the small community was actually rife with internal conflicts, which had their roots in family feuds that went back for generations. Lately there had been a few suspicious fires, and people were growing increasingly uneasy about the arson. It was unlikely their unease would lead to anything, Celia thought, because people there believed in keeping clear of matters that didn't concern them.

Celia, who had participated in several antisegregation marches in the 1960s, had learned never to assume that anyone shared her experiences or her views on anything. Thus, she wondered how the community would react to the play. She didn't know where these people stood on the issue of civil rights nor frankly, with the strife in Lone Pine, whether they had even given it much thought.

As she watched the play, Celia realized the teachers and students were more astute than she'd expected. Though the focus was on King's role as a civil rights leader, the dominant theme was his commitment to nonviolence.

At the end of the play, the student body stood on the stage and waited until the applause died down. Then, in a solemn voice, the boy who'd played Martin Luther King, Jr., spoke: "Like Dr. King—a man we have come to greatly admire and respect—the students of Lone Pine dream of a society where men and women strive to resolve their differences without violence and to live together in harmony.

Therefore, we will use the proceeds of tonight's ticket sales to dedicate a Peace Cross in the town square, to honor Dr. King and to remind us to settle our disputes peacefully. We hereby call on everyone in this community to do whatever they can to end the violence, and to follow this great man's example as a peacemaker. Please join us in this quest."

Celia and the rest of the audience sat in stunned silence. Then a thunderous applause shook the small Lone Pine Community School auditorium as an angel of peace from another time, another place, another battle, reached out to touch their hearts.

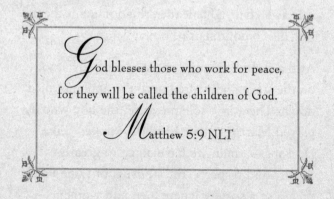

God blesses those who work for peace, for they will be called the children of God.

Matthew 5:9 NLT

Lord, send your angels and give me peace:
  Quiet as the shadows,
  Deep as the ocean,
  Still as the stars,
  Big enough to fill my heart,
  And mighty enough for all the world.

TAKING PART IN THE MIRACLE

Watching the morning news usually made Denise feel sad and sorry—sad for humanity and sorry she turned on the TV. But one morning the news brought a different story, one that left her with a spirit of hope and happiness. The story unfolded with a flashback to Sarajevo in 1992:

A mother and her two young sons sat huddled in a dark, cold basement. They looked hopeless, sad, at the end of their means. The father had been killed two months earlier while waiting in a line for bread, and the oldest son, 12-year-old Mirza, had lost his right leg while shielding his brother, Haris, from a grenade blast just outside the family's home.

A reporter spoke to the boy with crutches, and amid the nightmare of war, pain, and hunger, Mirza Kafedzic looked up at the journalist and said, "I just want a normal life for my family."

At that moment, a world away in the United States, a man who believed in miracles was watching the news of war-torn Bosnia. Phil Morgaman was moved when he heard the boy's words and decided right then that he had to do something about it. He began making telephone calls, hundreds of calls, in America and Europe, trying to reach the right people who could help him make things a little easier for this family. Again and again, he was told there was nothing he could do. But Morgaman was not one to give up. He believed not only that miracles could happen, but also that sometimes you get a chance to be part of someone else's miracle.

Through his determined efforts, Morgaman motivated countless people and organizations to help. Two Bosnian journalists risked their lives to find the family, and because of Mirza's injury, UN officials allowed their relief pilots to fly the family out of danger. In the United

States, doctors, clinics, churches, schools, and individuals banded together to provide the Kafedzic family with food, medical care, a place to live, and most importantly, friendship and a chance to rebuild their lives.

Ten years later, the family was thriving in south Florida, thanks to Phil Morgaman, his family, and the entire community. Both boys were now in college. Fitted with a prosthetic leg, Mirza could walk, run, and even play basketball. The boys love and look up to their "Uncle Phil." Like him, they too want to make a difference in someone else's life. "That's the kind of person I want to strive to be," said Mirza.

As Denise finished her coffee and left for work, she felt happier than she had for a long time and felt grateful she'd turned on the TV. Morgaman's incredible kindness to strangers renewed her belief in humankind, and also in the existence of angels—people here on earth who respond to strangers with loving kindness and offer help in times of need. As she drove to work, she marveled at how an angel rescued a small, shattered family and gave many other people a chance to take part in the miracle.

An angel spreads his glittering wings over us, and we say things like "It was one of those days that made you feel good just to be alive" or "I had a hunch everything was going to turn out all right" or "I don't know where I ever found the courage."

FREDERICK BUECHNER

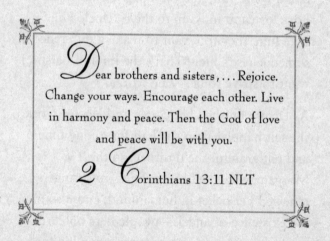

Dear brothers and sisters, . . . Rejoice. Change your ways. Encourage each other. Live in harmony and peace. Then the God of love and peace will be with you.

2 *Corinthians* 13:11 NLT

THE ANGEL WITHIN US

*God has chosen her as a pattern for other
angels. As you look at your own life, how might
you be an angel to others? How might you
pattern your life so as to inspire others to greater
heights in their own loving and giving?*

EPITAPH IN AN ENGLISH CHURCHYARD

>—•—>—•—<—•—<

*If we want to live as angels for other
people, we don't need wings and halos,
just loving attitudes. Being aware of other
people's needs, fears, dreams, and
heartaches, we can reach out as a loving
presence. We don't need to solve their
problems or change their lives as much as
we need to offer ourselves.*

STREET ANGEL

Afflicted with insomnia, Jim often walked the streets of the big city that was his hometown. Eventually, his wanderings took him farther into neighborhoods where he had not ventured before. At first, he was barely aware of his surroundings or the people he passed. One night, though, he realized with a start that the same people were leaning in the same doorways and bus shelters night after night. He looked more closely at their layers of worn-out clothing. They were homeless, a condition that Jim, a successful insurance salesperson, had only read about. He began to nod and say hello, and sometimes his greetings were returned.

One blustery March night, Jim came across a man he had seen several times on his walks. The man was slumped on the steps of an old building. On other nights, he had seemed friendly, but tonight he barely nodded when Jim said hi. In a flash, Jim thought the man may be weak from hunger. Jim dug through his parka pockets and found a candy bar. He offered it hesitantly, embarrassed that the candy looked like it had been in his pocket awhile. The man took it gratefully, thanking Jim so sincerely that Jim felt even worse that he didn't have more to offer.

From then on, Jim filled his pockets with candy and fruit and purposely directed his walks to the neighborhoods where he knew he would encounter hungry homeless people. Soon he was toting a backpack full of sandwiches and other easy-to-carry foods. Jim developed a regular route, and his new friends waited anxiously for his visits.

Somehow, the word got out that Jim had become a walking food pantry. Others offered to help. A grocer provided day-old bread and sandwich meat. Donations of more food as well as money trickled in.

Sometimes Jim didn't feel up to the journey, but he made his walk anyway, not wanting to let down his street friends. Before he knew it, he was feeding 100 people a night.

Not every journey went smoothly. Jim faced threats and, once, a knife-wielding mugger. A big man, Jim told his concerned friends, "I can take care of myself, but it's usually not necessary. I know that these people are suffering, and they act out of fear." The homeless individuals he was feeding thanked him, but Jim felt that he was the fortunate one to be able to help them.

Life on the streets was lonely, and occasionally the people wanted to talk even more than they wanted something to eat. Jim offered a handshake or a hug to anyone who seemed to need one.

Once in a while, Jim noticed that his efforts had made a difference. One night, a newer-model car pulled up next to him and the driver announced he'd been looking all over for Jim.

"Don't you recognize me?" he asked with mock indignation and handed Jim a check. "That's the money you lent me and more. Without it I couldn't have turned things around."

Friends marvel at Jim's seven-day schedule. Many ask what keeps him going. Jim turns his eyes upward and says simply, "I sincerely believe that he walks with me." Some nights

Jim's so weary he can barely finish his route. "You know," Jim comments with an easy smile, "I never have trouble sleeping anymore."

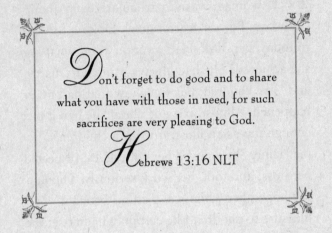

Don't forget to do good and to share what you have with those in need, for such sacrifices are very pleasing to God.

Hebrews 13:16 NLT

Today, it will be a privilege and a pleasure to do the work of angels.

The angels do your work, Father. I want to do it, too. You made me a person, not an angel. I can't fly through time or travel the universe, but I am willing to do whatever I can. Help me see your agenda and stick to the plan.

FIFTY REASONS TO FEEL LOVED

Marsha, who considered herself a plain woman, wasn't particularly vain about birthdays. But she wasn't much looking forward to today, her 50th. Half a century and what had she achieved? She had always wanted to marry and have children, but somehow that had never happened. Almost, but not quite. She had a nice enough job as an illustrator for a children's magazine. She enjoyed her colleagues, respected her boss, and took her work seriously. Though she hoped her whimsical pictures brought pleasure to children, she certainly hadn't set the art world on fire the way she had dreamed she would when she was 18.

Oh, well. She supposed the day would pass. She was grateful her coworkers didn't seem to know that her decade-breaker day was approaching. She could be as good a sport as anyone but had to admit she didn't like the idea of cards with memory-loss jokes and a sea of black balloons. When she arrived in her cubicle, she was surprised and intrigued to see a mountain of cards and a large package on her desk. Inside the package was a framed poster made by her coworkers, labeled, "50 Reasons We Love Marsha."

Written on the poster and cards were reminiscences of gestures and small kindnesses that Marsha had either taken for granted or forgotten about. Don mentioned how she always bought things she didn't even want from everybody's kids for school fundraisers. People who were hired after Marsha recalled that she was the first person in the office who had asked them to go out to lunch. It made Marsha smile, and even tear up a little, to see that Sara, a recent college graduate in an entry-level position, had written how much Marsha encouraged everyone's hopes and dreams, going out of her way to help make them come true. Had she? How? She didn't even remember that.

Several coworkers mentioned Marsha's smile, the one she was self-conscious about because her parents couldn't afford braces when she was a teen. The younger women in the office wrote that they considered her a mentor, and especially valued her infinite patience in showing them the ropes. Marsha could feel the beginnings of a blush tingling on her scalp, but she had to admit it felt good. The blush deepened as she went on to read about her contagious laugh, the malted milk balls she kept in a ruby-red cut-glass candy dish on her desk, her practical jokes, the hand-illustrated cards she gave for birthdays. She read about the funerals she had attended of coworkers' parents she had never met, her visits at the hospital whenever anyone had surgery, the nights she had worked late to help others meet their deadlines, and the way she often quoted Yoda from *Star Wars:* "There is no try, only do."

That night before bed, as she hung the precious poster on the wall, Marsha realized that nothing had really changed since morning but her attitude. She understood that she had been incredibly blessed to have had such a good and meaningful life so far. She went to bed eager to wake up the next day. She could hardly wait to start the next half century.

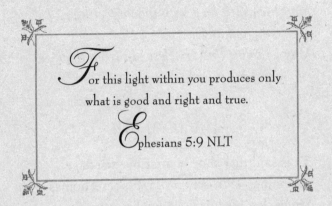

For this light within you produces only what is good and right and true.

Ephesians 5:9 NLT

God, I want to be an angel, but I'm not sure I fit the job description. I may not even have the prerequisites or experience to get hired. You may have plenty of others who could do the job better than I could. My heart is willing, though, and I can easily muster enthusiasm for the task ahead. I know you can work in me, so I'm asking for your spirit of encouragement, your special blessing. Help me to act like an angel and ask for no reward. Let your spirit be my spirit, so we can fly together!

May I learn to love with the perfect love of
   God and angels,
May I receive this priceless gift from them—
   and pass it on.

BELIEVE ME

It is said that shortly after his marriage,
famous 19th-century Irish poet Thomas
Moore left his lovely young bride for an
extended business trip. He eagerly returned
home weeks later and bounded up the steps to
his house. Anxious to become reacquainted
with his new mate, a startled Thomas was
greeted instead by the family physician.

"I have bad news, Sir," said the doctor. "Your
wife has been gravely ill and she asks that you
do not see her."

Thomas learned that during his lengthy absence
his wife had contracted smallpox. Although it
spared her life, the dreaded disease ruined her
dewy fresh, flawless skin, leaving deep pocks
and thick scars. She took a single, horrifying
look in a mirror, then ordered the shutters
pulled tight and the heavy drapes drawn,

leaving her in total darkness. She refused to let her husband see her marred face.

But Thomas ignored her command. He bolted up the stairs and threw open the doors. His wife's room was still and black inside. Feeling his way into the darkness, he fumbled to find the lamp.

"No! Not that. Oh, please, Thomas, don't light the lamp!" she beseeched him.

He hesitated, touched by the desperate, pleading voice.

"I beg you to leave, Thomas. You must not see me like this. Please go, go. Leave me here unseen."

Thomas did go. He calmly turned. He quietly walked from the room. He gently shut her door. And he strode directly down to his study where he spent the night writing. Thoughtfully, painstakingly writing. Not the poems for which he was known. This time, Thomas wrote a song. He labored to combine words and melody that expressed the fullness in his heart. Finally satisfied, he set it aside and slept.

The next morning, Thomas arose with the sun and raced up to his wife's room, where not even a weak ray of light penetrated the blackness. He groped his way to a chair.

"Are you awake, dear?"

"I am." Her voice sounded dismal. "But you must not ask to see me. Please, Thomas, do not press me."

"Then I will sing to you."

Thomas Moore began to sing. He sang to his wife the song he had composed the night before. It was a tender song. A song that expressed his thoughts; a song that declared his love; a song that still touches hearts today. He sang:

Believe me if all those endearing young charms,
Which I gaze on so fondly to-day,
Were to change by to-morrow, and fleet in my
    arms,
Like fairy-gifts fading away!
Thou wouldst still be adored, as this moment
    thou art,
Let thy loveliness fade as it will,
For around the dear ruin each wish of my heart
Would entwine itself verdantly still.

It is not while beauty and youth are thine own,
And thy cheeks unprofaned by a tear,
That the fervor and faith of a soul may be
   known,
To which time will but make thee more dear!
O the heart that has truly loved never forgets,
But as truly loves on to the close,
As the sunflower turns on her god when he sets
The same look which she turned when he rose!

And so it was, with love and insight flowing from his heart to his pen, that Thomas Moore inscribed words for his wife—words to comfort, words to reassure. And, in so doing, he created a message to inspire the world.

O that I were an angel, and could have
the wish of mine heart, that I might go
forth and speak with the trump of God
with a voice to shake the Earth.

THE BOOK OF MORMON, ALMA 29:1

Loving Lord, you have sent angels to your people on earth throughout eternity. Some brought messages of hope, others gave warning. Some angels helped to still a fearful heart or encourage the downtrodden.

>―◇―O―◇―<

Thank you for those people you have sent in my life who have been angels for me. Let me find ways to be an angel for others.

CHARITY BEGINS ON THE BEAT

The newspaper's feature writer was sick. Joe, a brash young reporter, had been pulled off his regular beat, the cop shop, to do a story. When his editor told Joe he had to get up early to go to a church and write about a free breakfast program for kids, Joe protested, "I can't do that sob sister stuff."

His editor replied with a steely glare. "Okay," Joe sighed. The next morning was bitterly cold, and Joe quietly cursed as he drove downtown. His ancient Honda was still chilly by the time he pulled up to the church. He could tell he was at the right place from the flock of children streaming into the door. Few wore hats or gloves. *Kids!*, he thought.

Once inside, a motherly African American, Marguerite, showed him around, absent-mindedly patting the children who darted up to hug her.

"Why are there socks in the box marked for gloves?" Joe asked.

"Ran out," she replied. "Socks work just as well." Marguerite interrupted herself several times to tend to the kids. "Hey, Devon," she called out, "one piece of bacon until we see how many children show up. You know the rules."

Marguerite squatted down to address a pale and silent little girl in a stained sweat suit. Her hair was lank and uncombed. "Hey, Melissa," she said. "We missed you yesterday. Was Mom sick?"

Melissa looked down.

"Did you go to school?"

The little girl continued to study the floor.

"Okay, honey," Marguerite said, "go get in line. We have donuts today."

Melissa's eyes lit up as she left to join the line.

"Alcoholic?" Joe asked Marguerite.

She nodded. "Melissa stays home to take care of the baby when her mom's sick."

"Been in treatment?" he questioned.

"Half a dozen times."

Then Marguerite went to help in the kitchen because a couple of volunteers hadn't shown up. Joe stood in line for stale donuts and ate with the kids. He tried to talk to Melissa, but when she turned her head he figured from his police beat experience that she had been abused by one of her mom's boyfriends.

When the children finished eating, they had left for the school across the street from the church. Moved by his visit, Joe wrote a check to the church for an amount equal to one month of his pay. He handed the check to Marguerite.

"Not a word or I put a stop order on it," he said wryly.

"Gotcha, honey," Marguerite said.

⤜⤳⤲⤛

Lord, I think I finally get it. You invest your spirit in me so that I can offer you to the world around me. Help me do this well. My hands and my heart are available to you even if I don't have wings and a halo. Amen.

I saw the angel in the marble and carved until I set him free.

MICHELANGELO

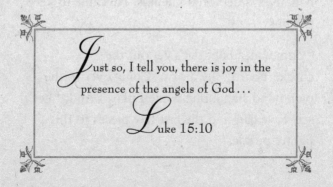

Just so, I tell you, there is joy in the presence of the angels of God...

Luke 15:10

*An angel can illuminate the thought and
mind of man by strengthening the power of
vision, and by bringing within his reach
some truth which the angel ... contemplates.*

FRAMED

Al devotedly visited Beverly every day. After all, until Beverly moved into Four Seasons Care Center, the couple never spent a night apart in all their 68 years of marriage. He needed to be with her, and she needed him.

"Al's here!" Beverly exclaimed each time he arrived. He was the only one she still recognized at this stage of her Alzheimer's disease. She was vague, disoriented, distracted, and idle unless he was there. He and Beverly had always deplored idleness. He came to keep her busy.

"Come on, honey, let's get out the checkerboard," he'd say. "Come over to the piano and sing along while I play." And, "Let's see if we can find the last few pieces to this jigsaw puzzle."

As long as he was there to challenge her, to engage her memory, and to guide her fingers, Beverly had her "good moments." The problem was Al still had lots of time on his hands when he visited. Something always interrupted them: baths, physical therapy, one-on-one assessments.

Al hated twiddling his thumbs. Like his dad had always said, "God promises no loaves to the loafer." Al had been raised on that principle as a kid and as an adult he'd practiced it as a busy optometrist. There was plenty to keep him occupied at home without Marie to help. But what could he do here, in this place where, like his wife, others had lost control of their memories, their minds, or their bodies?

Al walked down the hall noticing how many other residents were sitting in their rooms alone. He knew from his own experiences with Beverly that close friends and even family often didn't want to keep visiting someone who was in a care center. It was hard for them to see their loved ones so frail and vulnerable or to see someone they love dearly stare back without recognition.

"What's out there?" Al asked a man in a wheelchair, who was alone in his room looking out the window.

The man looked at Al in some surprise and then with a smile replied, "Same thing that's out there everyday—nothing much."

Al stepped into the room and introduced himself.

"Well, nice to meet you, Al. I'm Steve."

As the two men started to converse, Al saw in Steve the same positive change that happened in Beverly after spending a few minutes with her. *That's it!* Al realized. He spent so much time and energy thinking about Beverly that he hadn't thought about the other men and women living in the rooms around her. They, too, needed someone to remind them that they were still part of the world and didn't need to be alone and idle. Al would make sure to do that every day.

Life is short and we have never too much time for gladdening the hearts of those who are travelling the dark journey with us. Oh be swift to love, make haste to be kind.

HENRI FREDERIC AMIEL

God, you love us more than we can ever comprehend. You have even given your angels charge over us, to guide and protect us. Help us to be worthy of your love and the angels' care, that those we meet might consider us as bearers of angelic love.

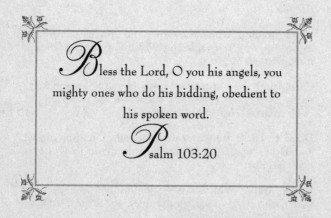

Bless the Lord, O you his angels, you mighty ones who do his bidding, obedient to his spoken word.

Psalm 103:20

Contributing writers:

Anne Broyles is co-pastor of Christ United Methodist Church in Malibu, California. She leads retreats on family and women's spirituality topics and is the author of many articles and books.

Rebecca Christian is a columnist, playwright, and radio commentator. She has contributed to *Heartwarmers: Grandmas Always Have Time* and *Heartwarmers: Moms Are the Best.*

Carol McAdoo Rehme is a writer and primary contributor to *An Angel by Your Side* and *Whispers from Heaven: For the Christmas Spirit.*

Carol Smith is an inspirational writer and holds a master's degree in religious education. She wrote and compiled the book *Angels—Heavenly Blessings.*

Diana L. Thrift is a writer who specializes in inspirational and nature topics. She has been a contributor to *Whispers from Heaven.*

Natalie Walker Whitlock is a columnist and freelance writer who covers a variety of topics. She is the coauthor of *Silver Linings: Friends.*